FOUNDATIONS FOR MORAL
RELATIVISM

J. David Velleman is a professor of philosophy at New York University. He is the author of four previous volumes, including *Self to Self* (Cambridge, 2006) and *How We Get Along* (Cambridge, 2009). He is a co-founder of the open-access journal *Philosophers' Imprint*.

Foundations for Moral Relativism

J. David Velleman

http://www.openbookpublishers.com

As with all Open Book Publishers titles, digital material and resources
associated with this volume are available from our website at:

http://www.openbookpublishers.com/product/181

ISBN Hardback: 978-1-909254-45-9
ISBN Paperback: 978-1-909254-44-2
ISBN Digital (PDF): 978-1-909254-46-6
ISBN Digital ebook (epub): 978-1-909254-47-3
ISBN Digital ebook (mobi): 978-1-909254-48-0
DOI: 10.11647/OBP.0029

Cover image: Egon Schiele, *Self-Portrait with Physalis* (1912). Wikimedia.org.

All paper used by Open Book Publishers is SFI (Sustainable Forestry
Initiative), and PEFC (Programme for the Endorsement of Forest
Certification Schemes) Certified.

Printed in the United Kingdom and United States by
Lightning Source for Open Book Publishers

for Kitty
my North Star

Contents

Acknowledgments

At a conference in the spring of 2012, I had the pleasure of meeting William St Clair, Chairman of the Board of Open Book Publishers. When he described the publishing model of OBP, I resolved at once that they must be the publishers of this book. I am grateful to OBP for taking it on, and especially to Alessandra Tosi and Corin Throsby for their work on its design and production. I am also grateful to my copyeditor, Katherine Duke, for her skillful attention to the manuscript and index.

Chapters III through V were presented as the Carl G. Hempel Lecture Series at Princeton University. They were then presented as the Hourani Lectures at the State University of New York at Buffalo. I am grateful to the philosophy departments at both institutions for honoring me with their invitations and for their hospitality during my lectureships.

A version of Chapter II was published under the title "Bodies, Selves" in *American Imago* 65 (2008): 405–426; before that, its title was "Artificial Agency". An early sketch was presented at a symposium on "The Psychology of the Self" at the 2007 Pacific Division meetings of the American Philosophical Association. Subsequent versions were presented to a philosophy of mind workshop at The University of Chicago; to a conference on "Ethics, Technology, and Identity" at the Centre for Ethics and Technology in Delft, the Netherlands; and to the philosophy departments of Union College, Syracuse University, the University of Vienna, the University of Leeds, and Brown University. Thanks to Linda Brakel, Imogen Dickie, Kalynne Pudner, and Kendall Walton for their valuable comments.

Chapter III was previously published in *Philosophical Explorations* on January 14, 2013, available online at http://www.tandfonline.com/ 10.1080/13869795.2012.756924. An earlier version was presented at a UCLA conference in honor of Barbara Herman. The commentator on that occasion was Carol Voeller. It was also presented as a ZENO Lecture at the University of Leiden, as the John Dewey Memorial Lecture at the University of Vermont, at a workshop on truth-telling and trusting at The University of Sheffield, and to the philosophy departments of Rice University and the University of Notre Dame. Thanks to audiences on all of these occasions, and also to Gabriel Abend, Alexandra Aikhenvald, Paul Boghossian, Frédérique de Vignemont, Imogen Dickie, Randall Dipert, Melis Erdur, Joan Manes, Bruce Mannheim, David Owens, Herlinde Pauer-Studer, Gunter Senft, Bambi Schieffelin, Will Starr, Sharon Street, Daniel B. Velleman, and the Mid-Atlantic Reading Group in Ethics (MARGE), especially members Paul Bloomfield and Kyla Ebels-Duggan. Thanks also to my anthropology professor at Amherst College, L. Alan Babb.

Versions of Chapter IV were presented to the philosophy departments of Colgate University, Rutgers University, Michigan State University, the University of Wisconsin — Milwaukee, the University of Vermont, Yale University, the University of Pennsylvania, Marquette University, and The City University of New York; to the Undergraduate Philosophy Forum at Columbia University; to the Phil/Sci workshop organized at the University of Vienna by Martin Kusch and Velislava Mitova; and to a workshop on normativity and truth at the University of Geneva. For help with this material, I am grateful in particular to K. Anthony Appiah, Paul Boghossian, David Braun, Stephen Darwall, Randall Dipert, Ken Ehrenberg, Don Herzog, Shelly Kagan, Alexander Nehamas, Herlinde Pauer-Studer, Gideon Rosen, and Matthew Noah Smith. Special thanks to the members of the Skype Reading Group in Ethics (SkyRGE) for repeated readings and discussions: David Owens, Nishi Shah, Matty Silverstein, and Sharon Street.

Chapter V was previously published in *Philosophical Explorations* on February 11, 2013, available online at http://www.tandfonline.com/10.1080/13869795.2013.767931. Bits of this chapter were presented at "The Pentagram of Love" at the 2008 Eastern Division Meetings of the American Philosophical Association. I am indebted to Rae Langton for a very helpful conversation about that version of the paper and for a subsequent exchange on this version. Discussions with Sharon Street helped me to abandon the first and begin on the second. Extensive written comments on the present version were provided to me by Ruth Chang, who organized the APA session. It was then presented at a colloquium organized by Nancy Yousef at The City University of New York. The lecture was also presented to the Department of Philosophy at the University of Miami and in a workshop on the ethics of family relationships at the University of Bern.

Chapter VI benefited from a helpful conversation with Sharon Street.

I. Introduction

There is no universally valid morality, only moralities plural, each having merely local validity. This much seems clear on first glance at the historical and ethnographic data. First impressions can be deceiving, though, and this one is troubling as well, so it calls for a second look. Ethnographers and historians can look again at its empirical sources;[1] a philosopher wants to look at its foundations. The philosopher asks: Can there be plural moralities of merely local validity?

There can of course be local *mores*. *Mores* are always specific to a culture or society or community.[2] But *mores* lack the obligatoriness, or binding force, of morality: one can be justified in ignoring or defying them. Also, *mores* include such trivial matters as the choice of a fork or the height of a hemline. Local moralities, by contrast, would have to make inexorable demands on unavoidable matters, despite being restricted to the members of a particular culture or society or community. Moral relativism must therefore explain how *mores* can have moral force and moral subject matter without being universal.

This explanation cannot invoke a universal obligation to conform to one's local *mores*, since moral relativism denies the existence of universal obligations. Nor can the explanation invoke extrinsic considerations such as a fear of social sanctions or a desire to fit in, since morality binds even those

---

1 I do not mean to imply that anthropologists have not done excellent work on the foundations of relativism. For an extremely clear and cogent characterization of moral relativism, see Richard A. Shweder, "Ethical Relativism: Is There a Defensible Version?", *Ethos* 18, no. 2 (1990): 205–218.

2 Throughout the book, I will use the term 'community' for a group of people living in proximity to one another and therefore obliged to interact with one another frequently. The term is less than ideal, but I know of none better. As the term is generally understood, the members of a community are bound together by more than proximity. Since one of my goals is to explain how they are bound together, however, I will use the term without that connotation, so as not to beg any questions. Moreover, communities have vague and porous boundaries, whereas I will speak as if they can be clearly individuated. In this latter respect, my use of the term is an idealization intended as an aid to theorizing.

DOI: 10.11647/OBP.0029.01

who do not care about these. Relativism must rather explain how *mores* can have the force and subject matter of morality all by themselves.

Philosophers may question whether I am really a relativist, for two reasons.

One reason is that I don't believe in faultless disagreement. Faultless disagreement would occur if one person accepted a proposition or principle and another person rejected it, without either one's being wrong. Faultless disagreement is impossible, though it's just the sort of impossibility that spurs philosophers to heroic measures on its behalf.

My concern is moral relativism in the real world, not in logical heaven. I want to explain how there can be multiple, locally valid moralities of the sort that there actually appear to be. That explanation need not show that there can be faultless disagreement between moralities; it may show instead that they do not even share enough common ground to disagree, and that it is therefore a moot question which one is right. If it's a moot question which of two moralities is right, then there is no adjudicating between them, and both remain standing — which is all that real-world relativism requires.

Of course, if 'morality' refers to a common set of pro-or-con questions on which different communities give different answers, then their views cannot be equally valid unless there is faultless disagreement. But the assumption of a common set of questions is already a form of universalism. It implies that communities agree about *how* to think, even if not *what* to think, about how to live. I believe that communities are more foreign to one another than that.

I see two obstacles to disagreement between moralities. One bar to disagreement is the lack of a shared taxonomy of actions. Actions are performed under descriptions, and act-descriptions are socially constructed, with the result that communities differ over the domain of things that can be done. If members of one community are choosing among options that members of another have never imagined, then the latter will have no opinion about the choice and no grounds for forming one.

A more profound bar to disagreement is that reasons for acting are essentially perspectival. What makes for a morality is not a set of answers to some universal questions but, as I have suggested, inexorable demands on unavoidable matters. Those demands come in the form of reasons for acting and reacting. I will argue that such reasons are perspectival in a way that prevents disagreement.

The challenge for a relativist who denies that communities disagree about a given set of moral questions is to show that there is still a shared topic

— namely, morality — on which they are, for that very reason, failing to disagree. In other words, such a relativist must show that different communities are talking about the same thing but not in sufficiently similar ways to clash head-on. I meet this challenge by showing that the *mores* of different communities can share general themes that we would call moral, which they address with a force that we would call moral, without agreeing or disagreeing on any particular moral issue.

In short, I regard moralities as variations on some themes — except that there is no fact of the matter as to which morality states the themes and which ones are variations. They are a family of diverse *mores* bound together (to vary the analogy) by family resemblance. For this reason, I do not offer a definition of what I mean by 'morality' or 'moralities'. I mean *that* family (you know which one it is). We should not be surprised that relativism rules out the possibility of giving a universal definition of morality.

My assertion of shared moral themes may be a second source of doubt about my credentials as a relativist. In order to show that there could be other moralities, I have to show that they would overlap enough with what we call morality to deserve the name, and then I seem to have found unavoidable convergence rather than unbridgeable difference.

Now, maybe local institutions similar enough to qualify as moralities will turn out to be one and the same institution adapted to local conditions, or maybe they will turn out to differ only by having different internal inconsistencies that will be ironed out in the long run. An optimistic thought, but it is no more than optimism. There is no *a priori* reason to think that differences among the world's many moralities would disappear if internal inconsistencies or external circumstances were factored out. Optimism must therefore be tempered with humility — that is, with the recognition that distant communities may never, not even ideally, converge.

Such humility is the main lesson of moral relativism. The mere possibility of multiple valid moralities should be enough to shake our certainty in having the absolute truth about morality, given that there may be no such thing.

The chapters of this book do not add up to a monograph, and their contents do not add up to a theory. They are self-standing essays that offer some foundational ideas for a version of relativism that would account for the cross-cultural and historical phenomena.

In Chapter II, "Virtual Action", I prepare the ground for my account of relativism by analyzing the construction of agency. I take as a model the construction of online agents in virtual worlds, where participants act with animated avatars as their online bodies. I argue that real agents are real-world participants acting, as it were, with flesh-and-blood bodies as their avatars. Both kinds of agent are designed, I claim, for social interaction of the sort required to pass a Turing Test of personhood.

In Chapter III, "Doables", I widen my view to the construction of action-types by members of a community. I argue that members of a community construct a shared taxonomy of actions because they need to make sense of one another and to one another for the sake of social interaction. The social construction of action-types results in differences that stand in the way of moral disagreement between communities.

The central chapter of the book is "Foundations for Moral Relativism", Chapter IV, which explains the construction of perspective-relative reasons that can underwrite the demands of local moralities. Although these processes leave no room for moral disagreement, I argue, they give application to a secular concept of progress. (This argument will raise further doubts about my credentials as a relativist.)

In Chapter V, "Sociality and Solitude", I offer a reason for thinking that human communities will tend to develop reasons that we can recognize as moral. I begin with the human capacity that makes possible the processes of action and interaction that I have discussed in previous chapters: I call this capacity objective self-awareness. I then argue that objective self-awareness is an essential, perhaps *the* essential, element of personhood, and that it is the object of many attitudes by which we value persons. Thus, the foundations of moral relativism, as I conceive them, are also foundations for pro-moral values.

Finally, in Chapter VI, "Life Absurd? Don't Be Ridiculous", I consider the claim that the truth of relativism would deprive life of its meaning. I argue that the possibility of progress, which I have asserted in Chapter IV, is sufficient to prevent life from being absurd.

II. Virtual Selves

Second Life

Most mornings, thousands of computer users log on to a virtual world called Second Life. Their computer screens show scenes of a nonexistent world, peopled by humanlike figures. Each user sees the world from the perspective of one of those figures, which is his avatar in the world and whose movements and utterances he controls through his computer keyboard and mouse. The other figures on his screen are being controlled by other users, all of whom witness one another's avatars doing and saying whatever their owners make them do and say. Through their avatars, these users converse, buy and sell things, and have all sorts of other humanlike interactions. (You'd be surprised.)

If you saw the virtual world of Second Life on your computer screen without knowing how the images were generated, you would take yourself to be watching an animated cartoon in which human beings, presumably fictional, were portrayed as doing and saying various things. Once you learned about the mechanics of Second Life, you would interpret the doings onscreen very differently. You would attribute them to unknown but real human beings who own and control the avatars that you see. And indeed the typical participant in Second Life attributes to himself the actions apparently performed by his avatar. What a participant causes his avatar to do in the virtual environment, he will report as his doing. "I went up to the professor after class", he may say, describing an encounter between a student-avatar that he controlled and an instructor-avatar controlled by someone else. In reality, the speaker went nowhere and encountered no one, since he was sitting alone at his computer all along.

DOI: 10.11647/OBP.0029.02

These self-attributions can be startling, given the differences between avatars and their owners. A young female avatar may belong to an older man, who may end up remarking, "For last night's party, I chose a tight dress to show off my figure." An able-bodied avatar may belong to a quadriplegic, who may then report, "I ran all the way."

The obvious interpretation of such remarks is that they have the status of make-believe. According to this interpretation, the animated figures on the speaker's computer screen are what Kendall L. Walton calls props in the context of pretend-play.[1] Such props include the dolls that children rock as if they were babies, the chairs that they drive as if they were cars, and so on. Just as a child might initiate a game of make-believe by pointing to a doll and saying, "This is my baby", the participant in Second Life may be taken as having pointed to his avatar while saying, "This is me."

Obvious though it may be, however, this interpretation makes an inference that I want to contest. Of course, when a participant says "I got dressed" or "I ran", whatever happened was not literally an act of dressing or running, since the clothes and bodies required for such actions do not exist. To this extent, the obvious interpretation is correct. But the interpretation goes on to conclude that the agency of this human participant is also fictional. When he claims to be the agent of the fictional actions that, according to the fiction, his avatar can be seen to perform, the obvious interpretation says that his claim must also be understood as fiction; I will argue that it is literally true. In my view, the participant literally performs fictional actions.[2]

---

1   Kendall L. Walton, *Mimesis as Make-Believe: On the Foundations of the Representational Arts* (Cambridge, MA: Harvard University Press, 1990). I should emphasize that the notion of a prop is all that I mean to borrow from Walton for the purposes of this chapter. I am not borrowing his theory of the representational arts.

2   This claim has the consequence that the semantics of our discourse about fiction cannot be represented by a sentential operator such as 'fictionally'. The fact that Shakespeare's play portrays the prince of Denmark murdering his uncle's advisor is sometimes expressed by philosophers of fiction with the statement "Fictionally, Hamlet murders Polonius." I will initially rely on this way of speaking merely as a matter of convenience. In the end, it will turn out to be insufficient to express my claim about virtual worlds. The claim that a human player performs a fictional action is not a claim to the effect that something is fictionally true. Nor is it merely the claim that the human player makes something fictionally true. It is the claim of a relation between an actual person and a fictional action, a relation that breaches the boundary between the real and the fictional worlds. Hence it does not consist in any purely literal or purely fictional truths nor in any combination of the two.

The problem with the obvious interpretation of virtual worlds is that it exaggerates the similarities between those worlds and make-believe. In order to explore the differences, I will use the label 'virtual play' for games such as Second Life, and 'pretend play' or 'make-believe' for the sort of game typically played by children. Please note, however, that these labels are not meant to be precisely descriptive.[3]

Pretend Play vs. Virtual Play

One respect in which virtual play differs from typical make-believe is that players cannot make stipulative additions or alterations to the fictional truths of the game. Their play is governed by a single, master fiction, namely, that they are viewing live images of a shared world. This fictional truth is given to the players, not invented by them, and it determines how all the other fictional truths will be generated in the course of their play: whatever is made to appear on the screens of participants will be what happens in the fictional world.

Aspects of determinateness

In pretend play, a child can say, "I'm a pirate, here is my ship, and you are my prisoner." Five minutes later, the pirate ship can be turned into a spaceship, and the prisoner into an android, by another declaration of the same form. The participants in virtual worlds can make no such stipulations.[4] In their

---

3 What I call virtual play involves some amount of pretending, and its characteristics can be found in games that are not virtual, strictly speaking, in that they do not depend on an information-based ontology. For example, fighting with paintball guns will turn out to be a case of what I call virtual play. In describing virtual play, however, I will confine my attention to the virtual-world participation that is typical of a deeply involved, fully committed player in a game such as Second Life, who spends a significant portion of his week "in world", under the guise of a single, persisting avatar with whom he identifies (in some sense that remains to be explained). My aim is not to generalize about all participants in virtual worlds of any kind; it is merely to explore what is possible by way of action in virtual worlds, by focusing on the case in which action is most likely to occur. In describing pretend play or make-believe, I will speak of the simplest and most familiar examples of the genre, the spontaneous and unregimented imaginative play of young children. I will use these terms to label opposite ends of what is in fact a continuum of possible games, in which the make-believe and the virtual are variously combined.

4 This statement is not quite true of text-based multiuser domains in which a player makes his avatar act by entering a description of what it is doing. Even here, however, such statements are limited to actions that the player's avatar is in a position to perform. Other

capacity as human participants in the game, they cannot say anything at all; they can speak only through their avatars. And by doing so, they can make true only the sorts of things that real people can make true by speaking. If a player wants a pirate ship, his avatar must build or buy one; if he wants a prisoner, his avatar must capture one; and he cannot turn his pirate ship into a spaceship unless his avatar carries out the necessary alterations.

A second difference between virtual worlds and the worlds of pretend play is their determinateness in proportion to the knowledge of the participants. What is true in a make-believe world includes only what the players have stipulated or enacted, plus what follows from those overt contributions; what is true in a virtual world is usually far more determinate than the players know or can infer.

Thus, when the children begin playing at pirates, the objects in their environment have no determinate roles in the fictional world of the game, and their characters have no determinate histories. If the children do not assign a fictional role to the coffee table, either explicitly or implicitly, then there is no fact of the matter as to what it stands for in the fiction. Usually, the players are on an equal footing as authors of the fiction, and so the facts of their fictional world are limited to what has been entered into the store of common knowledge among them, since secret stipulations would be pointless in a collaborative game.

By contrast, a virtual world has determinate features that outrun what is known to any of the players. Each player has to explore this world in order to learn what it is like, and he will then encounter others whose knowledge of the world is largely disjoint from his. The need to explore a virtual world interacts with the aforementioned necessity of instrumental action, since a player can explore the virtual world only by making his avatar explore it. He cannot learn about a part of the virtual world unless his avatar goes there. He sees only from the avatar's perspective, and he cannot see around corners unless the avatar turns to look.[5]

These differences between virtual and make-believe worlds extend to the nature of a player's actions. In either context, the behavior of an actual person makes it fictionally true that something is done by his

---

features of the world are not open to stipulation. In any case, my discussion is limited to graphical worlds.

5   These descriptions are subject to a slight but significant qualification. In some virtual worlds, each player occupies a perspective slightly behind and above his avatar, so that the avatar's body is within his field of view. I think it is not accidental that this perspective corresponds to one that is sometimes experienced in dreams.

counterpart, but what is made fictionally true by a player in make-believe is less determinate, and more dependent on stipulation, than what is made fictionally true by the player in a virtual world.

In the typical make-believe game of pirates, if one player pretends to stab another, there is no fact as to how much damage has been done until one of them makes the requisite stipulation or takes a relevant action, such as pretending to die. The difference between a graze and a fatal wound is not determined by the physical enactment of the blow. If the players fall to arguing over whether the victim is dead, they cannot examine the action for evidence; even a video replay would not settle the question. The players' behavior was therefore insufficient to determine whether a killing occurred, and the indeterminacy must be resolved by discussion among them.

This indeterminacy runs in both directions. Not only is it indeterminate what action a player has fictionally performed by means of a particular bodily movement; it is also indeterminate what bodily movement a player must employ in order to perform a particular fictional action. What must a player do in order to climb the rigging of his pirate ship? There is no skill or method of climbing fictional ropes. The bodily means are underdetermined, precisely because so many different movements might be stipulated to constitute the desired action.

In virtual play, however, determinate manipulations of keyboard and mouse are required as a means of causing particular movements on the part of an avatar, and those movements have determinate consequences in the virtual world. In order to bring about what he intends in that world, a player must make his avatar behave in ways that are effective under the "natural" laws governing the world, and he can do so only by providing input that will bring about such behavior, given the design of the user interface.

Role opacity

Yet a third significant difference between virtual and pretend play lies in the relation between the players and their roles. This relation differs in what I will call its opacity or transparency.

In pretend play, the make-believe characters are impersonated by actual children who know one another and see one another playing their roles. What a child chooses to do as a make-believe pirate is attributed both to the pirate, as his action within the fiction, and to the child, as his contribution to the game. The role of pirate is consequently transparent: it allows the player to show through. The transparency of the role even allows the player to emerge from it completely without any change of venue or medium. When the children start to argue about whether one pirate has killed the other, they implicitly lay down their fictional roles and argue as children: there is no suggestion that the pirates have decided to lay down their swords and "use their words" instead. But the children may be standing in the same places and speaking with the same voices as they did a moment earlier in their roles as pirates.

In virtual worlds, the actual players are usually unknown to one another: they interact only through their avatars. Even if the owners of different avatars know one another's identities, those identities are not on display in the virtual world; the players don't see one another's faces as they would in pretend play. Hence their avatar-identities are opaque.[6] There is no way for players to emerge from behind their avatars to speak or act as their actual selves. They can, of course, communicate with other players whose identities they know, but only in person or by e-mail or instant message or telephone, not in the venue or medium of the game.

Psychological engagement

These differences between virtual and pretend play produce one final difference, which involves the players' psychological engagement with the fictional world of the game. In make-believe, a player is aware of his power to invent the objects and events of the fictional world, and this awareness affects his attitudes toward them. His cognitive attitudes must conform at any point to the actions and stipulations made thus far, but they are not constrained to the same extent as beliefs would be constrained by reality. Instead of being reality-tested, like beliefs, these cognitive attitudes are tested against the incomplete fiction of the game, into which they can introduce additional details and further developments just by representing them and being voiced as stipulations. Hence these attitudes are only partly like beliefs while also being partly like fantasies. Similarly, the player's conative attitudes differ from the attitudes that he would have toward real

---

6   Although I noted earlier that paintball games qualify as virtual in my taxonomy, I am unsure whether they resemble online virtual games in this respect. Of course, the actual players are visible, unlike the actual players in a virtual world. But they are unable to set aside their fictional roles as combatants, since there are no "time outs" during which the fiction can be suspended. Hence their roles are transparent in some respects and opaque in others.

objects and events. A monster that he has made up, and is aware of being able to kill by means of further make-believe, does not frighten him as a real monster would.

In a virtual world, however, the players are aware of dealing with objects and events that, however fictional, are still not for them to conjure up or conjure away. These objects and events have the determinateness and recalcitrance characteristic of reality, and so the players tend to have more realistic attitudes toward them. The players' cognitive attitudes must conform to the truths of a world that is not of their invention, and that world can frustrate or disappoint them as their own fantasies cannot.

The players in make-believe generally invent the attitudes of their characters, fictionalizing about what those characters are thinking and feeling. If a player imagines that "his" pirate is angry or is coveting the treasure, he is not reporting his own feelings. Similarly, what he imagines his pirate to believe about the location of the treasure need not reflect his own beliefs; he may have no belief on the subject, since he may know that the treasure's fictional location has not been fixed.

In virtual play, by contrast, participants do not generally attribute attitudes to their avatars at all; they simply have thoughts and feelings about the world of the game, and they act on that world through their avatars but under the motivational force of their own attitudes. Players who send their avatars into unknown regions of the virtual world are genuinely curious about what they will find; they do not endow their avatars with a fictional curiosity to motivate their fictional explorations. Players themselves want the virtual items that their avatars buy — want to own them in the virtual world, that is, via their avatars — and they weigh the cost of those items against other uses for which they themselves foresee needing virtual dollars. Players whose avatars get married in the virtual world (and there are indeed virtual marriages) describe themselves as being in love, not as authoring a fictional romance. They do not experience themselves as artists inventing characters; they experience themselves as the characters, behaving in character, under the impetus of their own thoughts and feelings.[7]

---

7 At this point, one might object that a real person cannot be curious about a merely fictional landscape, nor desire merely fictional property, nor love a merely fictional spouse. Yet participants in virtual worlds insist that they do, and I am inclined to take their avowals at face value. Real curiosity about a fictional landscape strikes me as unproblematic. As I have explained, a virtual world has the determinateness and fixity characteristic of reality: there is a (fictional) fact of the matter as to what it is like in innumerable respects, and one can want to know such (fictional) facts. Desire for fictional things is

Virtual Agency

Consider now the intentions of a player with respect to the actions that result from his curiosity about the virtual world, his desire for some of its goods, or his love for another of its inhabitants. When he first joins a virtual world, the player finds it difficult to control his avatar, not yet having mastered the technique with keyboard and mouse. At this point, he can act with the intention of manipulating the keyboard and mouse in various ways, and with the further intention of thereby causing his avatar to do various things.[8]

As the player gains skill in controlling his avatar, however, manipulations of the keyboard and mouse disappear from his explicit intentions. He still controls the avatar by manipulating his keyboard and mouse, but only in the sense in which he types the word 'run' by moving his two index fingers. When he was just a beginner at typing, he still had to intend the movements by which he typed the word, but now those piecemeal movements have been incorporated into skills with which he can perform higher-level actions straightaway. He can simply decide to type 'run' without intending the means to that accomplishment, since his typing skills will take care of the means. (Indeed, he may have to type the word, if only in mid-air, in order to remember which fingers he uses to type it.) Similarly, the skilled player in a virtual world does not explicitly intend his manipulations of the input devices.

Even if a skilled player does not have explicit intentions to manipulate his keyboard or mouse, however, the possibility remains that he at least intends to control his avatar — say, to make the avatar walk and talk.

---

slightly more complex. The fictional world includes determinate property rights, which are vested in the user. Users can buy or sell virtual property in the real world (on eBay, for example), or they can exercise their property rights in the virtual world, via their avatars. Clearly, users can desire virtual property that they hope to sell in the real world. My point in the text is that they can also desire virtual property as such. Love for an entirely fictional character would be genuinely problematic, I think. But as I will explain, the characters in virtual worlds are not entirely fictional: they are chimerical creatures, compounded of fictional bodies and real minds. That such creatures can fall in love does not strike me as out of the question, for reasons that will emerge in due course.

8   Note that I am using the word 'intention' in a sense that is ambiguous between the "planning" attitudes analyzed by Michael Bratman and the "aiming" attitudes from which he distinguishes them (*Intention, Plans, and Practical Reason* [Cambridge, MA: Harvard University Press, 1987]). On the ambiguity of the term 'intention', see also Gilbert Harman, "Willing and Intending", in *Philosophical Grounds of Rationality: Intentions, Categories, Ends*, ed. Richard E. Grandy and Richard Warner (Oxford: Oxford University Press, 1986), 363–380.

Yet I think that the other features of virtual play favor the hypothesis that the player intends, not to make his avatar do things, but rather to do them *with* his avatar or to do them *as* his avatar or, more colloquially, simply to do them.

As we have seen, a virtual environment resembles reality in being both determinate and recalcitrant, confronting the player with facts that can be discovered and altered only by way of appropriate steps on the part of his avatar. In general, the player has no access to those facts *in propria persona*; he must deal with them in the opaque guise of his avatar, which can be neither penetrated nor circumvented by his actual self. Under these circumstances, intentionally manipulating the avatar would entail operating on the virtual world by an awkward remote control. The avatar would persistently stand between the player and the effects he wanted to bring about in the virtual world, like one of those glass-boxed derricks with which players try to pick up prizes in a carnival arcade.

This mode of operation would be highly disadvantageous. Intending to manipulate one's avatar so that it does one's bidding would be (to adopt a different analogy) like intending to maneuver one's tennis racket so that it hits the ball. And as any tennis player knows, trying to make the racket hit the ball is a surefire way of missing. Given that one must deal with the ball by way of the racket, one does best to treat the racket as under one's direct control, as if it were an extension of one's arm. And then one says, "I hit the ball with my racket", as one might say, "I hit it with my hand"; one does not say, "I made my racket hit the ball."

The skill of hitting a ball with a tennis racket is a modification of hand-eye coordination, which is a sub-personal mechanism. This mechanism computes and extrapolates the trajectory of a moving object and then guides the hand to intercept it at an angle and velocity that will produce desired results. None of this computation or guidance shows up in the subject's practical reasoning or intentions; the subject simply decides to catch something or hit something, and his hand-eye coordination takes care of the rest. In acquiring the skill of playing tennis, a player modifies the mechanism of hand-eye coordination to compute the relevant trajectories in relation to the head of his racket rather than his hand, and so he acquires racket-eye coordination, which is also a sub-personal mechanism.

So it is, I suggest, with an avatar. As one gains skill in controlling one's avatar, one acquires avatar-eye coordination. And then one no longer intends to operate on the virtual world by controlling one's avatar; one intends to operate with the avatar, as if it were under one's direct control.

One therefore intends to perform avatar-eye-coordinated actions in the virtual world, not real-world actions of controlling the avatar.

Whereas a tennis racket under one's direct control serves as an extension of one's arm, however, an avatar under one's direct control serves as a proxy for one's entire body: it is one's embodiment in the virtual world. Saying "I did it with my avatar" would therefore be like saying "I did it with my body" — something one rarely says, since "with my body" goes without saying whenever one says "I did it" in reference to a bodily action. That's why a player in the virtual world attributes the actions of his avatar directly to himself, just as he would the movements of his body.[9]

Combining the foregoing considerations, we arrive at the conclusion that the participant in a virtual world moves his avatar under the impetus of his own beliefs and desires about the virtual world, and he does so with intentions like the ones with which he moves his own body (and its prosthetic extensions) under the impetus of his beliefs and desires. Hence the player's relation to the avatar, though different from his relation to his own body in many respects, nevertheless resembles it in those respects which are relevant to his status as agent of his bodily movements.

When engaged in virtual play, in other words, a person really has a fictional body. Although the body itself is fictional — it is not really a body or even a real object of any kind — the player's relation to that fictional body is real, at least in the respects that are most significant for bodily agency, since it is directly controlled by intentions motivated by the player's beliefs and desires.[10] Hence the player is not speaking fiction when he calls his avatar "me". He is not strictly identical with the avatar, of course, but his first-person references to it are not meant to imply a strict identity anyway. If a rider in a packed subway car complains, "There's an elbow in my ribs", the answer might come back, "Sorry, that's me" — meaning "That's my elbow." Similarly, when a player points to his

---

9   One speaks of doing things "with my body" only when the entire weight or volume of one's body is involved, as in breaking down a door.

10   This claim is modeled on the claims made by Sydney Shoemaker, "Embodiment and Behavior", in *The Identities of Persons*, ed. Amélie Oksenberg Rorty (Berkeley: University of California Press, 1976), 109–137. It is also the implicit topic of Daniel C. Dennett, "Where Am I?", in *Brainstorms: Philosophical Essays on Mind and Psychology* (Cambridge, MA: The MIT Press, 1981), 310–323. Indeed, the present chapter can be read as a reprise of Dennett's paper, with avatars substituted for robots.

avatar and says "That's me", he means "That's my (fictional) body." And he is speaking the literal truth.

This equivalence can be restated in the other direction, as follows: Even if you never play video games, you already have an avatar by default; your default avatar is your body.

Synthetic Agency

The analogy between a person's body and an avatar suggests further similarities between virtual and real-world agency. I now want to explore those similarities by focusing on a notable feature of people's behavior in virtual worlds.

Participants in virtual worlds report that when acting with their avatars, they act in character. Rather than acting in their own characteristic ways, they act in ways characteristic of people like their avatars, who may differ from them in gender, age, race, physiognomy, and physique. Weaklings create muscle-bound avatars with which they swagger; wallflowers create ravishing avatars with which they seduce. If a woman's avatar is a ponytailed guy with a pack of cigarettes tucked in his sleeve and a guitar around his neck, then she acts like a jazz musician, even if she is a Wall Street banker. If her avatar looks like a Wall Street banker, then she behaves accordingly, no matter who she is. Indeed, participants report that the major attraction of living a "second life" is that, having adopted avatars different from themselves, they find themselves behaving like those different people rather than their real-world selves.

What explains this feature of virtual-world behavior? I believe that the explanation can be found by comparing virtual action to a kind of agency that is thoroughly artificial.

As long as an avatar is standing idle, it is indistinguishable from what is called a non-player character, or NPC — that is, a graphical figure whose behavior is controlled by software rather than by a human player. If the software behind an NPC is sufficiently sophisticated, it can generate behavior similar enough to that of a player-controlled character that other players may be unable to tell the difference. In Second Life, NPCs perform tasks of user support, for example, by answering routine questions from newcomers to the world. NPCs are examples of what might be called synthetic agency.

There is a literature on synthetic agents, divided into two segments. One segment discusses software programs that their designers describe as autonomous; I will describe these synthetic agents as rationally independent, so as to leave open the question of their autonomy in the philosophical sense of the term. The other segment of the literature on synthetic agents discusses what have come to be called believable agents, which are believable in that they give the impression of behaving like persons, even if they take nonhuman forms.

When a synthetic agent is rationally independent, it can carry out tasks without human direction or assistance. Like any software application, of course, this agent must be given instructions that "tell" it how to perform its function. But the function that its preprogrammed instructions tell it how to perform is the higher-order function of carrying out first-order tasks of some open-ended kind, for which precise steps are not specified in advance. Performing those tasks will require figuring out how to perform them, by adopting and prioritizing goals, generating and testing strategies, devising and revising plans, and so on.[11]

Rationally independent software agents can be fairly smart, giving the impression that they are not just calculating but also evaluating, strategizing, and learning. Hence the designer's description of them as autonomous is not entirely inapt. But they tend to come across as autonomous automata — smart and independent machines in which there appears to be nobody home.

Believability is at a premium in synthetic agents that must interact with real people. Consider, for example, a system designed by computer scientists at The University of Memphis to do the job of a Navy "detailer", who negotiates with sailors about where they will be posted at the end of their current assignment.[12] As the time for reassignment approaches, a sailor must email the detailer to learn about available openings, and the two of them carry on a correspondence with the aim of finding a good fit for the

---

11   One model for creating independent software agents is called the BDI model, whose initials stand for Belief/Desire/Intention. See Michael J. Wooldridge, *Reasoning About Rational Agents* (Cambridge, MA: The MIT Press, 2000). This model was in fact developed with the help of Michael Bratman's classic work *Intention, Plans, and Practical Reason*, but even models developed without reference to the philosophical literature resemble the BDI model in their focus on goals, deliberation, and planning.

12   See, e.g., S. Franklin, "An Autonomous Software Agent for Navy Personnel Work: A Case Study in Human Interaction with Autonomous Systems in Complex Environments", in *Papers from 2003 AAAI Spring Symposium*, ed. D. Kortenkamp and M. Freed (Palo Alto: AAAI, 2003), accessible at http://ccrg.cs.memphis.edu/papers.html.

sailor's skills, preferences, and family needs. In order to fill the detailer's shoes, the software needs an impressive degree of intelligence, including the ability to process natural language and the ability to optimize multiple parameters at once. But the detailer must also perform the very human task of negotiation — advising, cajoling, bullying, and ultimately persuading the sailor to accept an assignment. The Navy therefore wanted the system to seem like a human detailer, so that the sailor would forget that the party at the other end of the correspondence was a computer. In short, the Navy wanted a software agent that was not just rationally independent but also believable.

The pioneering work on believable agents was done by a group of computer scientists at Carnegie Mellon University, in what was known as the Oz Project. To find the secret of creating synthetic agents that were believable, they looked to the "character-based" arts, such as acting and, more to the point, cinematic animation as developed in the studios of Walt Disney and Warner Brothers. A. Bryan Loyall, whose doctoral dissertation was the first extended treatment of the subject,[13] found several recurrent themes in the reflections of these "character" artists.

The artists seemed to agree that the first two requirements of believability are the expression of a personality and the expression of emotion. The notion of personality here includes traits of the kind that social psychologists list under that heading, such as extroversion or introversion, but it also includes distinctive styles of speech and movement, specific predilections and tastes, and other characteristics that endow each person with what we call his individuality. As for the expression of emotion, it is now widely recognized as a necessity by designers of believable agents, including the ones who designed the automated Navy detailer. That system was equipped not only with models of memory and consciousness but also with a model of the emotions, which were manifested in its behavior. For example, the automated detailer was programmed to be impatient with sailors who contacted it at the last moment before needing a new assignment.

The third requirement of believability, after the expression of personality and emotion, is what Loyall terms "self-motivation", defined

---

13 See A. Bryan Loyall, *Believable Agents: Building Interactive Personalities*. Dissertation presented to the School of Computer Science, Carnegie Mellon University (1997). See also Michael Mateas, "An Oz-Centric View of Interactive Drama and Believable Agents", in *Artificial Intelligence Today: Recent Trends and Developments*, ed. Michael J. Wooldridge (Berlin: Springer-Verlag, 1999), 297–328.

as the agent's acting "of his own accord" rather than merely responding to stimuli. Loyall says that self-motivation is achieved when behavior "is the product of the agent's own internal drives and desires",[14] but the example he cites does not bear out this gloss. The example comes from Disney animators Frank Thomas and Ollie Johnston, who describe self-motivation in more colloquial terms as "really appear[ing] to think" — a description that is even less informative:[15]

> Prior to 1930, none of the [Disney] characters showed any real thought process. [. . .] The only thinking done was in reaction to something that had happened. Mickey would see [something], react, realize that he had to get a counter idea in a hurry, look around and see his answer, quickly convert it into something that fit his predicament, then pull the gag by using it successfully.
>
> Of course the potential for having a character really appear to think had always been there [...], but no one knew how to accomplish such an effect. [. . .] That all changed in one day when a scene was animated of a dog who looked into the camera and snorted. Miraculously, he had come to life!

Surely, what made this dog "really appear to think" was not that he manifested "internal drives and desires" or the results of deliberation. Indeed, deliberation in the service of desires is precisely what was manifested in the behavior attributed here to Mickey Mouse as an illustration of not yet appearing to think. The sense in which the dog "really appeared to think" is that he did not just manifest his internal states; he appeared to be aware of them and to be expressing that self-awareness. Indeed, he appeared to be expressing it *to* the audience, hence attempting to communicate.

Loyall lists several additional requirements of believability, but I will focus on only one, which subsumes and integrates the requirements mentioned thus far. Loyall calls it "consistency of expression":[16]

> Every character or agent has many avenues of expression depending on the medium in which it is expressed, for example an actor has facial expression, body posture, movement, voice intonation, etc. To be believable at every moment all of those avenues of expression must work together to convey the unified message that is appropriate for the personality, feelings, situation, thinking etc. of the character. Breaking this consistency, even for a moment, causes the suspension of disbelief to be lost.

---

14   Loyall, *Believable Agents*, 20.
15   Frank Thomas and Ollie Johnston, *Disney Animation: The Illusion of Life* (New York: Abbeville Press, 1971), 74.
16   Loyall, *Believable Agents*, 22.

Thus, the believable agent must produce behavior that not only expresses his personality, thoughts, emotions, and self-awareness but also does so coherently, in the sense that the features expressed and the behaviors expressing them fit together into what Loyall calls a "unified message".

Real-World Believability

The need for a unified message would explain why participants in a virtual world act in the character of their avatars. Acting in character helps to make their avatars believable, by unifying the avatars' behavioral "message" with the message conveyed by their appearance.

But why is unification necessary for believability?

Think of it this way. When participating in a virtual world, a player undergoes an updated Turing Test. Turing imagined having a subject communicate via teletype with an unseen interlocutor who was either a second person or a computer.[17] Turing said that if the computer could fool the subject into thinking that he was communicating with another person, it would qualify as intelligent. As it happens, a similar test confronts the computer that controls non-player characters in a virtual world. Ideally, NPCs would behave in ways indistinguishable from the actions of avatar-embodied persons — though as of yet, NPCs are far from ideal.

What is usually overlooked about the Turing Test is that it tests intelligence only indirectly, by testing for the appearance of personhood, and that it can serve in both respects as a test for human beings as well as for machines. The performance of the machine is judged by being compared with that which would be expected of a person, and there is no reason why the performance of a human cannot be judged similarly.

In fact, you have probably taken a test just like Turing's. If you have exchanged instant messages with someone over the Internet, then you have used Turing's setup. In order to use it successfully, you had to send messages that your interlocutor would interpret as coming from a person rather than from a "zombie" computer churning out spam or a virus commandeering his machine. And if you have participated in a virtual world, then you have faced the task of acting with your avatar in ways that the other participants would interpret as the actions of an avatar-embodied person rather than an NPC.

---

17   Alan Turing, "Computing Machinery and Intelligence", *Mind* 59, no. 236 (1950): 433–460.

In order to pass the Turing Test of instant messaging, you have to send unified messages — that is, messages containing intelligible discourse that expresses consequent thoughts and coherent feelings. You send such messages so that they will be understood. But even a spam-bot sends intelligible messages: what makes you more believable than a spam-bot?

What distinguishes you from a spam-bot is that in trying to make yourself understood, you also betray an awareness of participating in a project of mutual understanding. You give your interlocutor to understand how you have interpreted what he has said, and you adapt what you say not only to what he has said but also to what it indicates about his interpretation of what you said before. By such means, you engage in a subtle form of social interaction in which the interactants adjust their messages so as to communicate successfully.

That's what the animated dog seemed to be doing when he snorted. The self-awareness that he appeared to express included the awareness of being seen by viewers who would interpret his snort as an expression of disdain. He looked as if he was communicating disdain, not just expressing it — as if he was expressing it, that is, with the intention of being so understood, hence as if he could be asked, "What do you mean by that?" His believability was thus achieved by more than a unified message; it was achieved by the appearance of sending a message with an awareness of how it might be received. His believability was achieved, in other words, by the appearance of sociality.

In face-to-face interaction, the messages sent and received are visual as well as verbal. What people do and say is interpreted in the context of how they look, and incongruities create misunderstandings. When a down-and-out musician asks about the Dow Jones average, we wonder whether he is putting us on. If he uses the jazz idiom 'bad' while dressed as a banker, he is sure to be misinterpreted. That's why players in virtual worlds unify their behavior and appearance: they are engaged in self-presentation for the purpose of social interaction. And because they are clearly prepared to suit their behavior to that purpose, they are believable.

But avatars are just the virtual bodies of real people, who act with them as they act with their real-world bodies. Does the similarity end there? Do people need to be believable only when acting virtually? After all, people unify their behavior with their appearance in the real world as well. Cut the musician's hair, dress him in a suit, give him a briefcase, and he will begin to act less like a musician and more like a banker. Give the banker a ponytail and he will begin, as we say, to let down his hair.

What's more, the dressed-up musician won't just act like a banker; he will begin to think and feel like a banker too. We call some people suits not because they wear suits and not just because they act like people who wear suits; they grow into their suits and thereby become "suits".

What follows is that the participant in Second Life, wearing his avatar like a suit, should come to have the thoughts, feelings, and, yes, personality of his avatar. Having the body of someone who can coherently feel confident in being aggressive — or coherently feel seductive or argumentative or whatever — he develops the corresponding traits, and then he animates his avatar with them and with the appropriate thoughts and feelings. This philosophical inference is confirmed by players in Second Life. They don't say, "In Second Life, I look like a nebbish and I act as if I am shy"; they say, "In Second Life, I *am* a nebbish and I *am* shy."

A character in Second Life is thus a chimerical creature in which a fictional, virtual-world body is joined to a literal, real-world mind. That real mind holds a self-conception of the hybrid creature to which it belongs, a creature whose personality, thoughts, and feelings it can know introspectively, unify among themselves and with his appearance, and communicate directly through its fictional body. Of course, the same mind holds a self-conception of a real-world human being to whom it belongs, but that self-conception is different: it is the conception of a different self. Two distinct creatures, one wholly real and one partly fictional, can be literally animated by one and the same mind, for which they help to constitute different selves.

III. Doables

Right now I am writing a philosophical essay about the sociology essay "On Doing 'Being Ordinary'", by Harvey Sacks.[1] The thesis of this brilliant essay (Sacks's, not mine) is that no matter what we do, we are doing something else in addition, namely, being ordinary. By "being ordinary", Sacks means doing something that is ordinarily done in a situation like ours, conceived as a situation ordinarily encountered by people like us, conceived as people of some ordinary kind. I am a philosophy professor, an ordinary sort of person to be. Even if I held the Extraordinary Chair in Philosophy (I don't), such a chair would be an ordinary sort of position for a professor to hold. And an ordinary sort of thing for a professor to do is to write an essay about a topic that he finds somewhat out of the ordinary, though not too far out.

Sacks puts his point like this:

> [T]here is an infinite collection of possibilities, of things to do, that you could not bring yourself to do. In the midst of the most utterly boring afternoon or evening you would rather live through the boredom in the usual way — whatever that is — than see whether it would be less or more boring to examine the wall or to look in some detail at the tree outside the window. (415–416)

In other words, there are ordinary ways of doing "being bored" — flipping unseeingly through an old magazine, staring unhungrily into the fridge — and when you are bored, you do it in one of those ways.

Another example:

> Among the ways you go about doing "being an ordinary person" is to spend your time in usual ways, having usual thoughts, usual interests, so that all you have to do to be an ordinary person in the evening is turn on the TV set.

---

1 *Structures of Social Action: Studies in Conversation Analysis*, ed. J. Maxwell Atkinson and John Heritage (Cambridge: Cambridge University Press, 1984), Chapter 16.

DOI: 10.11647/OBP.0029.03

> Now, the trick is to see that it is not that it *happens* that you are doing what
> lots of ordinary people are doing, but that you know that the way to do
> "having a usual evening," for anybody, is to do that. (415)

The reference to TV in this passage may seem to suggest that Sacks is talking
about being mundane or even inane. But he thinks that the task of being
ordinary confronts you in the course of even the most exotic episodes:

> [W]hether you were to have illegitimate experiences or not, the characteristic
> of being an ordinary person is that, having the illegitimate experiences that
> you should not have, they come off in just the usual way that they come off
> for anybody doing such an illegitimate experience.
>
>   When you have an affair, take drugs, commit a crime, and so on, you
> find that it has been the usual experience that others who have done it have
> had. [. . .] Reports of the most seemingly outrageous experience, for which
> you would figure one would be at a loss for words, or would have available
> extraordinary details of what happened, turn out to present them in a
> fashion that has them come off as utterly unexceptional. (418)

Although Sacks speaks here of "having experiences", the passage makes
clear that he means "exploits" or "adventures". Sacks is saying that if you
pass up an evening of TV in order to rob an all-night grocery, you will still
do "robbing an all-night grocery" in the ordinary way. (You've seen it on TV.)

A Version of Moral Relativism

In order for anyone to aim at doing what's ordinary, there has to be
something that is ordinarily done, which is whatever is done by others,
who, according to Sacks's thesis, are also aiming to do what's ordinary.
Hence everyone has to converge on a repertoire of ordinary actions that
isn't defined in advance of everyone's converging on it. Ordinariness is
socially constructed, and constructing it is a classic coordination problem.

   Because ordinariness is socially constructed, it is also local, in the sense
that it is relative to some population of agents who interact regularly,
usually because they live in one another's vicinity. What's ordinary in New
York or Omaha is not the same as what's ordinary in Ramallah or Singapore,
as everyone knows. One way to think of this phenomenon would be to
imagine a domain of actions — or, more accurately, action-types — from
which different communities[2] select different subsets on which to converge

---

2   While using the term 'community', I acknowledge that it is problematic. All of the
   alternative terms ('culture', 'society', and so forth) are problematic as well. There aren't

as the ordinary set. I will argue that this conception of the coordination problem would be mistaken, because there is no neutral domain of actions from which a community can select. In constructing what's ordinary, a community also constructs the domain of action-types.

The result is that communities can find themselves unable to disagree about what should be ordinarily done, because they differ with respect to what is doable: there is no neutral domain of action-types from which they choose what to do. What's more, action-types are invented, and there is no domain of inventable action-types from which communities can choose which ones to invent, much less disagree about such choices. Insofar as they can disagree about which action-types to invent, they disagree just by living differently, each converging on ordinary choices from among its own, socially constructed domain of doables.

This obstacle to disagreement extends to morality. Disagreement about morality is disagreement about what may or may not be done, and so it requires agreement about what is doable. For communities with different domains of doables, the question what may or may not be done is therefore moot.

Now, the nature of moral disagreement is the issue between moral relativists and their critics. Some think that the issue, more specifically, is whether moral disagreement can be faultless, in the sense that both parties to the disagreement are right. In my view, moral relativists should not rest their case on the possibility of faultless disagreement; they should rest it instead on the impossibility of disagreement altogether. Both of two parties can be entitled to stick to their moral views not because both are right but rather because it is a moot question which one is right, so that there is no moral question to adjudicate. Relativism requires only that there be no judicable question between moral views.

My goal in this chapter is to explain the construction of different practical domains by different communities. My explanation will be that the social construction of doables is governed by the same forces that produce the phenomenon of "doing 'being ordinary'", as described by Sacks. I'll conclude by returning to the implications for moral relativism.

---

well-defined communities or societies or cultures. When we theorize about them, we are simplifying. But I think that the simplification is warranted as an idealization for the purpose of theorizing.

Ethnomethodology

Sacks belonged to a group of sociologists who adopted the name of ethnomethodologists, because they sought to catalog the "methods" of ordinary life. As the name suggests, ethnomethodologists modeled themselves on anthropologists, for reasons explained by one of Sacks's co-authors, Emanuel Schegloff:[3]

> [A]nthropologists had had good reason over the course of the development of their discipline to wonder what some "natives" were "doing" by conducting themselves in a certain way, for example, by talking in a certain way. Both linguistic obstacles and so-called "culture differences" could pose quite sharply the problem of "recognizing actions," and then the analytic problems of describing what those actions were and how they were done or accomplished. [. . .]
>
> [. . .] [T]he same sort of attention to, and description of, actions in one's own culture never had quite the same resonance, even in anthropology. The actions were "transparent" to comembers of the culture, even naming them by action names might appear a bit arch and scholastic. Even more so was this treatment accorded accounts of the practices, rules, or mechanisms by which these actions were done. They just "were" invitations, requests, promises, insults, and so on.

This passage should ring a bell for philosophers, who know that we never detect what "just is". Our observations are informed by concepts of what there is to be observed — concepts of observables. Schegloff was pointing out that we act under concepts of what there is to do — concepts of doables.[4]

There is an important difference between observables and doables, however. The fact that observation is informed by concepts does not rule out the possibility that some of those concepts are more faithful than

---

3   Emanuel A. Schegloff, "Confirming Allusions: Toward an Empirical Account of Action", *American Journal of Sociology* 102, no. 1 (1996): 162–163.

4   On the individuation of options, see also Matthew Noah Smith, "Practical Imagination and its Limits", *Philosophers' Imprint* 10, no. 3 (2010): http://www.philosophersimprint. org/010003/. Of course, it won't come as news to philosophers that an action is always performed under a description. But the phrase 'performed under a description' is potentially misleading, because it means different things to the agent than it does to an observer. An observer sees a bodily movement and considers various descriptions under which it might have been performed. But the agent didn't choose among different descriptions for that particular bodily movement; he chose among different descriptions to enact. And the bodily movement by which he enacted his chosen description was determined, at the most basic level, by sub-agential skills stored in his brain and body. So even if there is a neutral substrate of movement that can be variously interpreted, that substrate is irrelevant, indeed invisible, from the agent's point of view; from the agent's point of view, there are merely act-descriptions to realize.

others to the structure of the world: there may be better and worse ways of articulating what we see, because the world itself may be articulated — may have joints at which some concepts carve it better than others. By contrast, which actions there are depends on which action concepts figure in people's intentions. We talk about "taking" an action, as if we were picking an apple from a tree, but actions don't antecedently exist in nature, waiting to be picked. What we call taking an action is actually *making* an action, by *en*acting some act-description or action concept. Which actions we can make depends on which descriptions or concepts are available for us to enact.

Individuals can sometimes invent new things to do, but invention is the exception rather than the rule. An agent cannot invent an entire ontology of actions from scratch; for the most part, he must choose from a socially provided repertoire of action concepts. Just as he sees things of kinds that he has been taught can be seen, so he does things of kinds that he has been taught can be done. As the sociologist Ann Swidler has argued, a person's culture provides him not so much with values and ends as with a "toolkit" of possible actions:[5]

> People do not build lines of action from scratch, choosing actions one at a time as efficient means to given ends. Instead, they construct chains of action beginning with at least some pre-fabricated links. Culture influences action through the shape and organization of those links, not by determining the ends to which they are put.

These socially provided links for possible chains of action are what I interpret Sacks to mean when he speaks of what is ordinary, and they are what I will mean by 'doables'.

It is not just a shortage of time or energy or imagination that prevents an individual agent from venturing outside the predefined range of doables. The shared ontology facilitates mutual understanding and cooperation. This point was emphasized by Alfred Schutz, a philosopher from whom the ethnomethodologists drew inspiration.[6]

---

5 "Culture in Action: Symbols and Strategies", *American Sociological Review* 51, no. 2 (1986): 277.

6 Alfred Schutz, "Equality and the Meaning Structure of the Social World", *Collected Papers II*, ed. Arvid Brodersen (The Hague: Martinus Nijhof, 1964), 237. See also "Common-Sense and Scientific Interpretation of Human Action", *Philosophy and Phenomenological Research* 14, no. 1 (1953): 19–20, 25–26, and "Concept and Theory Formation in the Social Sciences", *The Journal of Philosophy* 51, no. 9 (1954): 268.

On the one hand, I have — in order to understand another — to apply
the system of typifications accepted by the group to which both of us
belong [. . .]. On the other hand, in order to make myself understandable
to another, I have to avail myself of the same system of typifications as a
scheme of orientation for my projected action.

What Schutz calls a "typification" is simply the concept of a typical action —
something ordinarily done. One draws on a shared system of typifications,
according to Schutz, in order to understand what others do and to do
things that others can understand.[7]

That taxonomies of doables are socially constructed can be inferred
from cultural differences in action concepts. A commonplace among
linguists, for example, is that some cultures have only one verb for the
actions that we discriminate as *eating* and *drinking*;[8] indeed, some have
a single verb for *eating*, *drinking*, *smoking*, and *kissing*.[9] In such cultures,
taking in through the lips is a more salient action-type than taking in
smoke; in our culture, taking in smoke is more salient: we don't even have
a verb for the other.

Social construction extends even to the level of bodily movements, for
the simple reason that parts of the body are differently individuated
in different societies.[10] The social anthropologist Edwin Ardener offers

---

7   Note that Schutz's thesis doesn't apply to solitary actions: you don't choose recognized
    ways of being bored in order to make yourself interpretable to others. (If others were
    around to interpret you, you might not be so bored.) I would say that you choose
    recognized ways of being bored in order to be interpretable to yourself.

8   Anna Wierzbicka, "All People Eat and Drink. Does This Mean That 'Eat' and 'Drink' are
    Universal Human Concepts?", in *The Linguistics of Eating and Drinking*, ed. John Newman
    (Amsterdam: John Benjamins, 2009), 65–89. For a general discussion of whether there are
    lexical universals, see Kai von Fintel and Lisa Matthewson, "Universals in Semantics",
    The Linguistic Review 25, no. 1–2 (2008): 139–201.

9   William A. Foley, *Anthropological Linguistics: An Introduction* (Malden, MA: Blackwell,
    1997), 28; Borut Telban, "The Poetics of the Crocodile: Changing Cultural Perspectives
    in Ambonwari", *Oceania* 78, no. 2 (2008): 227. As Randall Dipert has pointed out to me,
    there are certainly universal categories of action. Even if *ingesting* is not among them,
    a category such as *self-moving*, or *locomotion*, probably is. But such categories are universal
    in the sense that every community has action concepts that fall within the category, not
    in the sense that every community has the category itself as an action concept.

10 See the special issue on terms for body parts in *Language Sciences* 28 (2006). See also
    Drid Williams, "Taxonomies of the Body", *Journal for the Anthropological Study of Human
    Movement* 1, no. 1 (1980): 1–11.

an example of how different taxonomies of the body generate different taxonomies of action:[11]

> Let us consider the shaking of hands in England and among the Ibo of south-eastern Nigeria. In both languages there are apparently intertranslatable terms for the gesture (Ibo *ji aka*). Although *aka* is usually translated "hand" the boundaries of the parts concerned are, however, quite different. The English "hand" is bounded at the wrist. The Ibo *aka* is bounded just below the shoulder. [...] The more open-gestured nature of the Ibo handshake compared with the English handshake is linked in part to this difference of classification. For the English-speaker the extreme, "formal" possibility of presenting an only slightly mobile hand at the end of a relatively stiff arm becomes a choice reinforced by language. For the Ibo-speaker, even if that is a possible gesture it has no backing from language.
>
> Consistently shaking hands alone, with articulation only at the wrist, might therefore seem to the traditional Ibo a slightly incomprehensible restriction of movement, equivalent perhaps in flavour to being, in the English case, offered only two or three fingers to shake. From the opposite point of view, to the English speaker "shaking hands" and "arm-grip" are two *kinds* of greeting. To the Ibo they are degrees of intensity, demonstrativeness, of warmth, of "the same" greeting.

Ardener goes on to explain that although helping can be described in both languages as "lending a hand", requests for a helping hand are met differently. In circumstances that call for the literal proffer of a hand, an Ibo may proffer a forearm even if his (English) hand is available. The way an Ibo lends a hand may therefore strike an English speaker as cold — he wonders, "Why won't you give me your hand?" — which is how the English speaker's handshake strikes an Ibo, who wonders, "Why do you give me just the tip of your hand?"

Ardener suggests that even the categories of *action* and *behavior* are socially constructed. Among the Ibo, he claims, all generic terms for behavior carry connotations of social approval or disapproval. So there is only good or bad behavior for the Ibo, not behavior *simpliciter*.[12]

---

11 "Social Anthropology, Language and Reality", in *Semantic Anthropology*, ed. David Parkin (New York: Academic Press, 1982), 4–5.

12 "'Behaviour': A Social Anthropological Criticism", *Journal of the Anthropological Society of Oxford* 4, no. 3 (1973): 152–154, p. 153, reprinted in *Journal for the Anthropological Study of Human Movement* 10 (1999): 139–141, and in Ardener, *The Voice of Prophecy and Other Essays*, ed. Malcolm Chapman (Oxford: Blackwell, 1989), 105–108.

The Social Construction of Speech Acts

Consider next the example of speech acts. I choose speech acts for two reasons. First, they are actions that have been extensively taxonomized by philosophers, in speech-act theory. Second, the hierarchy of speech acts can seem to be universal, at least in its overall shape, and so the work of constructing it is easily overlooked. Although the acts of *filibustering* and *excommunicating* are obviously constituted by social practices, the acts of *asking* and *asserting* do not immediately strike us as culture-bound. Indeed, John Searle claims that the fundamental illocutionary forces — the assertive, the directive, the commissive, the declarative, and the expressive — are natural kinds that exhaust the possible uses of language.[13] In other words, the fundamental doables of verbal communication are simply there to be done, according to Searle. Yet it turns out that Searle's inventory of illocutionary forces may be culture-bound after all, as is our taxonomy of the acts that exert those forces.

Commissives among the Ilongot

Searle's inventory of illocutionary forces was first challenged by the anthropologist Michelle Rosaldo in an account of speech acts among the Ilongot people of the Philippines.[14] According to Rosaldo, neither the expressive nor the commissive categories have clear instances among the Ilongot. The closest approximation to commissives such as promises among the Ilongot neither express the same attitudes nor incur the same consequences as promises in English. They are rather oaths nominating calamities to befall the speaker if he fails to follow through. Such failures do not occasion guilt or apology:

> Repeatedly, I was outraged to find that friends who had arranged to meet and work with me did not appear at the decided time — especially as they would then speak not of commitments broken, or of excuses and regrets,

---

13   John R. Searle and Daniel Vanderveken, *Foundations of Illocutionary Logic* (Cambridge: Cambridge University Press, 1985): "Illocutionary forces are, so to speak, natural kinds of uses of language . . ." (179); "[A]s far as illocutionary forces are concerned there are five and only five fundamental types and thus five and only five illocutionary ways of using language" (52).

14   "The Things We Do With Words: Ilongot Speech Acts and Speech Act Theory in Philosophy", *Language in Society* 11, no. 2 (1982): 203–237.

but of devices (such as gifts) that might assuage the generally unexpected and disturbing anger in my heart. To them, it mattered that I was annoyed (a dangerous and explosive state), but not that someone else, in carelessness, had hurt and angered me by failing to fulfill commitments I had understood as tantamount to promises. (218)

In this culture, the way to give people grounds for counting on one's future action is to make oneself vulnerable to harms if one should disappoint them. One alters one's own incentives, in other words, without making any commitment to others, so that if one lets them down, one will need only to watch out for oneself and to assuage their disappointment.

Evidentials

Whereas the Ilongot fail to exercise illocutionary forces that are included in Searle's inventory, other communities exercise illocutionary forces that Searle's inventory lacks. Consider languages that use grammaticized rather than lexical evidentials — that is, grammatical means of indicating the speaker's epistemic relation to what is said. In these languages, the speaker's epistemic position is indicated by word-endings rather than by words or phrases. One ending may be used for statements of what the speaker has witnessed firsthand, another for what the speaker has heard from others, a third for what is generally known in the community, a fourth for what the speaker infers or intuits. In some languages, such evidentials are mandatory; that is, a speaker must always add a word-ending that indicates his epistemic position.

Whereas an English speaker says, "He's out hunting, I'm told", a speaker of Quechua says, "He's out hunting-*si*", '-si' being the reportative evidential in his language.[15] In the Amazonian language Matses, evidentials are mandatory in all past-tense statements, which include all statements about absent parties.[16] If a man is asked how many wives he has and they aren't present, he will answer with a statement whose grammatical evidentials

---

15 Martina T. Faller, *Semantics and Pragmatics of Evidentials in Cuzco Quechua*, Ph.D. dissertation submitted to the Department of Linguistics, Stanford University (2002); available at http://personalpages.manchester.ac.uk/staff/martina.t.faller/documents/Thesis.pdf.

16 David W. Fleck, "Evidentiality and Double Tense in Matses", *Language* 83, no. 3 (2007): 589–614.

can be translated into English only with lexical evidentials, like this: "There were two (last time I checked)."[17]

The first thing to say about languages with mandatory evidentials is that they do not have a speech act corresponding to our bare assertion. It is impossible, in these languages, to put forward a proposition as true without indicating how it is known to be true. In place of our bare assertion, they have several speech acts, which we might call testifying, reporting, speculating, and the like.

By the same token, we do not have speech acts afforded to speakers by languages with evidentials. We can of course say that what we are asserting is known firsthand, by intuition, or whatever, but we thereby insert material about our sources into the truth-conditions of our statement, whereas evidentials need not contribute to truth-conditions. When an English speaker adds the words "I'm told" or "reportedly" to an assertion, he not only indicates his epistemic relation to what is asserted; he also implies that a report of it has been made. One can therefore challenge him by saying, "That hasn't been reported." By contrast, a reportative evidential in Quechua can mark a statement as hearsay without yielding the further implication that it was heard, and so the challenge "That hasn't been reported" would misfire. The reportative evidential thus makes possible a speech act that is not available to speakers of English.

Indeed, it has been claimed that the reportative evidential in Quechua produces a speech act whose illocutionary force does not fit into Searle's taxonomy. In addition to leaving the truth-conditions of a statement unchanged, an evidential can lack the force of an epistemic modal. In Quechua, "He's out hunting-*si*" indicates a lack of certainty on the part of the speaker, as would the English statement "He may be hunting", but the Quechua statement is co-assertible with "He isn't hunting", whereas "He may be hunting" is not. And unlike "He may be hunting", the Quechua statement is co-assertible with "I know he isn't hunting" as well. Thus, Quechua speakers can say "He's out hunting" without implying that it may be true, that it is compatible with what is known, or that it has been heard, and yet in a tentative register reserved for hearsay. An evidential like the Quechua '-si' can thus generate a speech act that has the illocutionary force of "presenting" a proposition without vouching for its truth, actual or

---

17   *Ibid.*, 596. Obviously, this English translation carries implicatures that (one hopes) weren't present in the original. Whether the Matses answer can be translated without such implicatures is a difficult question.

epistemically possible — an illocutionary force that isn't accommodated by Searle.[18] Once again, the individuation of speech acts turns out to be culture-bound.[19]

Grice's maxims

Genres of assertion unknown to English speakers also appear in cultures where Grice's conversational maxims are said not to hold. In Malagasy society, for example, assertions are designed to be strategically uninformative, for various cultural reasons.[20] Life is generally lived in the open, and exclusive knowledge is therefore a rare commodity, possession of which confers prestige on the knower. There is also a risk of losing face if one's claims turn out to be false. Consequently, speakers go out of their way to convey less information than they could conveniently convey. Asked where someone is, a speaker will say, "In the market or at home", despite knowing which is the case.[21] Asked when someone will be at home, a speaker will say, "If you don't come after five o'clock, you won't find him", a circumlocution designed to be less informative than saying that the person will be in after five. Speakers use indefinite descriptions for people whose identity they know, so that a speaker who sees his own mother at the door may say, "Someone is here."[22] Hence "Someone is here" does not implicate that the speaker doesn't know who.

---

18 Faller, *Semantics and Pragmatics*. A similar proposal has been made for the reportative evidential in Korean: Kyung-Sook Chung, "Korean Evidentials and Assertion", *Proceedings of the 25th West Coast Conference on Formal Linguistics*, ed. Donald Baumer, David Montero, and Michael Scanlon (Somerville, MA: Cascadilla Proceedings Project, 2006), 105–113.

19 For an attempt to explain the use of evidentials (among other linguistic phenomena) in terms of cultural values, see Daniel L. Everett, *Don't Sleep, There Are Snakes: Life and Language in the Amazonian Jungle* (New York: Pantheon, 2008). As Daniel B. Velleman has pointed out to me, some English utterances come close to having a presentational force: "Take, for instance, the claim that he's out hunting." Yet even this utterance differs from the Quechua, since its fundamental force is directive, so that it has a world-word direction of fit. The response "No, let's not consider it" would be in order.

20 Elinor Ochs Keenan, "The Universality of Conversational Postulates", *Language in Society* 5, no. 1 (1976): 67–80. For an opposing argument, see von Fintel and Matthewson, "Universals in Semantics", 189. Von Fintel and Matthewson say that Keenan's argument is, to their knowledge, the only attempt to challenge the universality of Grice's maxims. I would argue that the examples I am about to cite in the text — examples of conventional uncooperativeness in conversation — have similar implications for Grice.

21 See also the quotation from Geertz, at note 28, below.

22 Keenan, "The Universality of Conversational Postulates", 73. As Daniel B. Velleman has pointed out to me, these utterances are not counterexamples to the Gricean maxim if

A more extreme phenomenon has been observed in cultures where the paramount values are honor and prestige.[23] According to an ethnography of an Egyptian village, conversation among the inhabitants is often a matter of negotiating a common ground that is more attuned, in the first instance, to social norms other than truthfulness:[24]

> Fairly transparently false assertions can still be effective in shaping the future course of a conversation because in most cases they are immune from challenge for reasons of politeness — showing respect not only for the other's honesty but also for their authoritativeness and soundness of judgement. There may be mutual knowledge that an assertion is false, while yet speakers cooperate on treating it as if true, or at least valid, for immediate conversational purposes ('valid' as with opinions one respects but disagrees with). But there has to be left open some possibility, however remote, that the assertion could be true, for the pretence to be workable; otherwise it slips over into irony [. . .].
>
> These regularities reveal that villagers are — and need to be — highly sensitive to issues of truthfulness and the concomitant sanctions, and to where truthfulness is and is not to be expected. They have a name for the type of speech where it is not expected: *kala:m* '(mere) words/talk', and it is freely acknowledged as occurring in a wide range of situations.

Kala:m is the name of an assertoric genre that does not seriously aim to be true but is not fictional, either, and is nevertheless permitted.[25] Conversely,

---

they intentionally flout it in order to establish the speaker's superiority — as if to say, for example, "Someone is here, but I'm not going to tell *you* who it is." But Keenan's description indicates that uninformativeness is conventional in the language, not exceptional in a way that would convey such a message.

23 See Richard F. Gombrich: "Lying is bound to be frequent in a culture much concerned with the preservation of status [. . .] and dignity [. . .] — saving face; the most trivial matter which might in any way appear discreditable to the speaker is concealed almost as a matter of course" (*Precept and Practice: Traditional Buddhism in the Rural Highlands of Ceylon* [Oxford: Clarendon Press, 1971], 263).

24 Rachael M. Harris, "Truthfulness, Conversational Maxims and Interaction in an Egyptian Village", *Transactions of the Philological Society* 94, no. 1 (1996): 41.

25 The villagers say, on the one hand, "We live with two faces", and on the other, "The English don't lie" (*ibid.*, 35 and 43, respectively). Here is a similar report, of a remote Greek village where honor and prestige are similarly valued:

In the village the word for lies, *psemata*, is used much more freely, with less emotional intensity, and with a milder pejorative connotation than Americans use the English word. "Let's tell a few more lies and then go home," a man once remarked jovially near the end of a social evening. To accuse someone of mendacity is not the gross insult it is in the United States; it may be meant as a statement of fact in a situation in which, in village expectation, it would not be unusual for a person to attempt some deception.

Ernestine Friedl, *Vasilika: A Village in Modern Greece* (New York: Holt, Rinehart and Winston, 1962), 80. See also Juliet du Boulay, "Lies, Mockery and Family Integrity", in

the Trobriand Islanders have a formula that means "Now I'm speaking the truth" — a formula that is not usually invoked, so that most indicative utterances can be retracted, if necessary, as having been *sopa*, or unserious.[26]

Untruthfulness

Among the Mopan Maya, the only word translatable as "lying" is *tus*, which carries no connotation as to the speaker's knowledge or intention:[27]

> There exists no other candidate lexeme in Mopan for the notion of "lying" or "stating falsehood," and the translation "lies, lying" is the only one ever offered for this form by bilingual Mopan speakers. Harshly or mildly applied, a negative connotation is always present to some degree in uses of this word. A characterization of another's utterance as *tus*, however, is based exclusively on the perceived truth value of expressions and not on the intentional or belief states of the speaker. This is so even when the speaker merely translates the opinions or repeats the words of another [...]. Accordingly many cases of expressions that might be categorized elsewhere as "errors" are condemned in Mopan as *tus*.

According to Clifford Geertz, the Javanese use the word *étok-étok* to mean "proper lying", which is not quite the same as our "white lie". An informant explained it to him like this:[28]

> He said: "Suppose I go off south and you see me go. Later my son asks you: 'Do you know where my father went?' And you say no, [you] *étok-étok* [that] you don't know." I asked him why should I *étok-étok*, as there seemed to be no reason for lying, and he said, "Oh, you just *étok-étok*. You don't have to have a reason."

Geertz elaborates:

> When we tell white lies, we have to justify them to ourselves even though the justification be weak. [. . .] For the Javanese [. . .] it seems, in part anyway, to work the other way around: the burden of proof seems to be in the direction of telling the truth. The natural answer to casual questions, particularly from people you do not know very well, tends to be either a vague one

Mediterranean Family Structures, ed. J.G. Peristiany (Cambridge: Cambridge University Press, 1976), 389–406.

26 Gunter Senft, "The Case: The Trobriand Islanders vs H.P. Grice: Kilivila and the Gricean Maxims of Quality and Manner", *Anthropos* 103 (2008): 139–147.

27 Eve Danziger, "The Thought that Counts: Interactional Consequences of Variation in Cultural Theories of Meaning", in *Roots of Human Sociality: Culture, Cognition and Interaction*, ed. N.J. Enfield and Stephen C. Levinson (New York: Berg, 2006), 260. References omitted.

28 *The Religion of Java* (Glencoe, IL: The Free Press, 1960), 246 (interpolations are mine).

("Where are you going?" — "West") or a mildly false one; and one tells the truth in small matters only when there is some reason to do so.

In some Lebanese circles, speakers of Arabic puff themselves up, and put others down, by passing off out-and-out falsehoods, which are admitted after the fact to be lies, or *kizb*.[29] In order to have the desired effect on the relative status of speaker and hearer, these falsehoods must eventually be revealed, and so they are not exactly the same as lies in the English-speaker's sense, but because they are so consequential in social terms, they are not exactly the same as "leg-pulling" or "April Fools'" jokes, either.[30]

Russian has two words for lying: *lozh*, which denotes an out-and-out lie, and *vranyo*, for which English has no equivalent. *Vranyo* is not exactly bullshitting, not exactly fibbing, not exactly joshing, not exactly telling tales. Here is an example:[31]

> I was once present when a USSR-domiciled Russian visitor to England spoke to a British host about a Russian *émigré* known to both of them. According to the visitor, one of the *émigré*'s sons had recently returned to Moscow after a stay in Paris; had published a book of which the exact title was given; had changed his name; had undergone various other adventures. The host listened with a straight face, thus preserving the conventions, though he was a close friend of the family concerned and knew that every word was untrue. Did the narrator realise that he had been identified as purveying *vranyo*? Yes and no.

The purveyor of *vranyo* does not quite expect to be believed. He does count on not being unmasked — on receiving a straight-faced hearing — but he also prefers aesthetic appreciation to naive credence.[32] It is even unclear whether he thinks that he is telling untruths. Dostoyevsky put it like this: "You have told such fantastic stories [. . .] that, though you have started to believe in yourself half-way through your story (for one always does begin to believe in oneself half-way through a story), nevertheless when you go

29   Michael Gilsenan, "Lying, Honor, and Contradiction", in *Transaction and Meaning: Directions in the Anthropology of Exchange and Symbolic Behavior*, ed. Bruce Kapferer (Philadelphia: Institute for the Study of Human Issues, 1976). On the meaning of '*kizb*', see also Harris, "Truthfulness, Conversational Maxims and Interaction".

30   See Eve E. Sweetser, "The Definition of *Lie*: An Examination of the Folk Models Underlying a Semantic Prototype", in *Cultural Models in Language and Thought* (Cambridge: Cambridge University Press, 1987), ed. Dorothy Holland and Naomi Quinn, 62. Sweetser claims, on the basis of fairly narrow cross-cultural evidence, that there is a core concept of lying that is universal.

31   Ronald Hingley, *The Russian Mind* (New York: Charles Scribner's Sons, 1977), 78.

32   *Ibid.*, 87.

to bed at night and have enjoyable memories about the pleasant impression made on your listener, you suddenly pause and remark involuntarily, 'Heaven, what rubbish I talked.'"[33]

Now, you may say, "But *kala:m, kizb, étok-étok,* and *vranyo* are just practices that we English-speakers don't happen to have. So what?" Here's what: These practices affect the individuation of speech acts. For both speakers and hearers of Russian, there are two ordinary types of untruthfulness, both of which would count as lying in English. If the Russians' *vranyo* is a type of action that we don't happen to have, then by the same token our lying is an action-type that they don't quite duplicate, either.[34] The same point applies to the Javanese, with the additional note that *étok-étok* and *vranyo* are different from each other, too.

I would argue that these forms of untruthfulness also strain Searle's taxonomy of illocutionary forces. In the practices that I have just described, propositions expressed in indicative sentences are not put forward simply as true or as to be believed. In some cases, they are put forward as entries into a common ground that may have no use beyond the present interaction. In other cases, they are moves in a conventionally sanctioned bluffing game, put forward as maybe true, maybe false, to be believed at one's own risk. I question whether these utterances have assertoric force.

There may even be cultural differences in the conceptualization of null speech acts — that is, acts of not speaking. In Anglo-American culture,

---

33 This passage can be found in "Something About Lying", from *The Diary of a Writer*, trans. Boris Brasol (New York: George Braziller, 1954), 133–142. I have substituted Hingley's translation (83). Hingley translates Dostoyevsky's title as "A Word or Two About *Vranyo*".

34 Here are a few further examples. The linguist Anna Wierzbicka writes, "There are many languages which have no exact equivalent of the word *warning* and which have, instead, words for modes of communication which have no equivalents in English. For example, Japanese has the word *satosu*, which combines some of the components of the English concept codified in the word *warning* with some other components: an assumption that the speaker has authority over the addressee, the intention of protecting the addressee from evil, and good feelings toward the addressee [...]. In English, the assumption of authority is encoded in verbs such as *order* and *forbid*, but it is never combined (lexically) with the intention to protect. [...] English doesn't have any verb which would combine authority, responsibility, and care [...]. " ("A Semantic Metalanguage for a Crosscultural Comparison of Speech Acts and Speech Genres", *Language in Society* 14, no. 4 (1985): 494). As Wierzbicka remarks, it may make no sense to talk of "'questions in Eskimo', 'commands in Burundi', or 'blessings and curses in Yakut'", because "English words such as *question, command,* or *blessing* identify concepts which are language-specific" (Wierzbicka, "All people eat and drink", 492).

silence is strenuously avoided in social situations, especially among strangers newly introduced, but for the Western Apache, "silent co-presence" is a way of socializing, especially among strangers, so that hosts and guests may sit silently for the first half-hour of a visit.[35] This community affords its members an act of sociable silence that is not available to Anglo-Americans.

One wonders, then, whether the Western Apache lack a precise correlative to the Anglo-American action-type of *speaking*, just as the Ibo lack a correlative to mere *behavior*. Or perhaps it is only *speaking up* that has no correlative among the Apache — at least, none without a tinge of the Anglo-American *interrupting*.

Why Construct Ordinariness?

Of course, part of the reason why speech is constrained by the local repertoire of speech acts is that speech acts call for uptake: you cannot use Quechua evidentials with hearers who don't understand the language. But the fact, which was noted by Schutz, is that you need uptake for most of what you do. It's imperative that others be able to interpret not just your speech but your behavior in general, so that they know how to interact with you — or how to avoid interacting with you, for that matter.

Navigating a crowded sidewalk requires you to let others understand what you are doing and even what you are feeling. Are you strolling aimlessly, rushing for a light, pausing at a store window, stopping to beg? All of these actions belong to a socially constructed ontology that must be shared by agent and interpreter if mutual understanding is to be attained.

If you want to ride the subway in New York, you'd better know how to make yourself understood — not necessarily in English, which is of limited utility, but in the behavioral vocabulary of crowding in, brushing past, reaching around, stepping aside; sprinting as opposed to chasing; nudging as opposed to jostling. When you come to New York, speak the local language of action: do not improvise.

---

35   Keith H. Basso, "'To Give Up on Words': Silence in Western Apache Culture", *Southwestern Journal of Anthropology* 26, no. 5 (1970): 213–230. See also Karl Reisman, "Contrapuntal Conversations in an Antiguan Village", in *Explorations in the Ethnography of Speaking*, ed. Richard Bauman and Joel Sherzer (Cambridge: Cambridge University Press, 1989), 112–113; and Ned Searles, "'Why Do You Ask So Many Questions?': Dialogical Anthropology and Learning How Not to Ask in Canadian Inuit Society", *Journal for the Anthropological Study of Human Movement* 11, no. 1 (2000): 47–64.

Think of the situation in which you realize that you have been staring at a point in space that has turned out to be occupied by someone else's face. You have carelessly let him think that you were staring at him, and now you have to convey that you weren't staring, because you didn't even see him, though you obviously saw him think that you were staring, and so you somehow have to convey that his thinking so was the first thing you saw. Then again, whether the person thinks you are staring at him will depend on whether he thinks that he has somehow led you to think that he is seeking attention, since an invited gaze is not a stare. If he thinks he might have seemed to be trying to catch your eye, then he may wonder whether you are paying attention rather than staring — in which case, he will make a show of staring at his feet, so as to convey that he isn't putting on a show, except for that one. The entire interaction requires a shared taxonomy of gazes.

Joint intentions

The need for a shared taxonomy of actions is intensified by the prevalence of joint intentions in human affairs.[36] As Margaret Gilbert has explained, you and I are in a position to speak of "our" doing something only if each has formed an intention that's conditional on the other's and only if we have common knowledge of those intentions.[37] Each must intend to do his part provided that the other intends likewise, and both must know that they have these intentions, and know that they know, and so on. This configuration of attitudes is most easily brought about by an exchange of words — "I'm willing if you are", "Then I'm willing, too" — but it can also be brought about tacitly, and tacit joint intentions are virtually ubiquitous, even where the resulting collaboration is not evident.

When I walk on a city street, I intend to leave the other pedestrians alone, provided that their intentions toward me are similar. I do not intend to leave them alone if they intend to interfere with me, nor even to leave them alone if they intend to leave me alone no matter what my intention toward them might be. If they intended to leave me alone even if I decided

---

36 See Herbert H. Clark, "Social Actions, Social Commitments", in Enfield and Levinson, *Roots of Human Sociality*, 126–150.

37 "Walking Together: A Paradigmatic Social Phenomenon", *Midwest Studies in Philosophy* 15 (1990): 1–14. I discuss this phenomenon in "How to Share an Intention", *Philosophy and Phenomenological Research* 57, no. 1 (1997): 29–50, reprinted in *The Possibility of Practical Reason* (Ann Arbor, MI: MPublishing, 2009).

to stare at them, or to take shelter under their umbrellas, or to dart into a taxi they have hailed, I might be tempted to do those very things. My intention toward them is therefore contingent on their having a similarly contingent intention toward me.

These intentions are common knowledge among us. We haven't exchanged explicit commitments: we haven't said, "I'm willing to leave you alone, provided that you intend likewise toward me." But we have implicitly signaled our intentions by our behavior. We avoid looking at one another too long, standing too near, following too closely, speaking or gesturing in one another's direction, and we do so in a way that is both defensive and deferential. None of us is certain of the others' intentions, but we are fairly confident, and our confidence is justified, with the result that, if vindicated in the event, it will turn out to have constituted common knowledge. We therefore satisfy the conditions for jointly intending to leave one another alone. Whereas some people jointly intend to walk together, we pedestrians jointly intend to walk apart.

Joint intentions require a shared taxonomy of actions. Indeed, they require a taxonomy that is not only shared but known to be shared — a taxonomy that is common knowledge. Each participant in the intention must know what the other intends; know that the other knows what he, the first knower, intends; and so on. Such knowledge is possible only if there is common knowledge as to the doables that can be intended.

Scenarios

Many of these joint intentions are intentions to participate in socially shared scenarios of standard interactions. Roger Schank and Robert Abelson argue that a robot would need to know many such scenarios in order to simulate an intelligent agent.[38]

---

38 Roger C. Schank and Robert P. Abelson, *Scripts, Plans, Goals, and Understanding: An Inquiry Into Human Knowledge Structures* (Hillsdale, NJ: Lawrence Erlbaum Associates, 1977). Schank and Abelson use the term 'script', which strikes my ear as implying that actions and utterances are mandated with more specificity than Schank and Abelson actually have in mind. I prefer the term 'scenario', which suggests a greater degree of indeterminacy, leaving room for improvisation. 'Scenario' is the term that was used for the standard plot outlines on which performers improvised in the Commedia dell'Arte tradition, and it was adopted by some of the originators of Chicago "improv" theater. (See R. Keith Sawyer, *Improvised Dialogues: Emergence and Creativity in Conversation* [Westport, CT: Ablex Publishing, 2003], 20 ff.) Where Schank and Abelson speak of scripts, and I speak of scenarios, Erving Goffman speaks of "routines" (*The Presentation of Self in Everyday Life* [New York: Anchor Books, 1959], 16 *et passim*). Sawyer discusses

Schank and Abelson's favorite example is the restaurant scenario, which can be pictured as a flow diagram of how a visit to a restaurant typically unfolds. Either you must wait to be seated — in which case, you may or may not be asked whether you have a reservation — or you are permitted to seat yourself; then you wait until someone brings a menu, or tells you what's available, or both; then you are left to deliberate; then the server arrives, and the diners take turns stating their choices from the available items, leaving out condiments, which are already on the table, and dessert, which is ordered later; and so on. Even if you knew that restaurants are places to eat, you would have trouble extracting a meal from one of them if you didn't know how the scenario goes. If you didn't know the scenario, of course, you might ask for directions at the door, but you would then have to know the "asking for directions" scenario.

To say that you know the scenario is to say that you are following the same flow diagram as everyone else. If you have mistakenly walked into the home of someone holding a private dinner party, you won't get very far with the restaurant scenario. As soon as the host holds out his hand for a welcoming handshake, you'll know that something is wrong. When you enter a restaurant, you begin the restaurant scenario because you believe that everyone else will follow the same scenario, and they follow suit because they believe likewise of you.

There are even scenarios for deprecated interactions (Sacks's "illegitimate experiences"). In order to pull off a mugging, you have to let the victim know he is being mugged, so that he will play his part.[39] When he surrenders his wallet and you take it, the two of you will thereby enact a handoff, according to a scenario that you jointly intend to enact: it takes two to hand over a wallet. If you're the jumpy type, you may shout, "No false moves!", meaning "Stick to the scenario!" or, as Sacks might put it, "Be ordinary!"

Scenarios for social interaction usually have their own entries in the taxonomy of actions: ordering a meal, welcoming a guest, shaking hands.

---

the variable specificity of scripts, scenarios, or routines in his *Creating Conversations: Improvisation in Everyday Discourse* (Cresskill, NJ: Hampton Press, 2001). For a recent philosophical discussion of scripts, see Cristina Bicchieri, *The Grammar of Society: The Nature and Dynamics of Social Norms* (New York: Cambridge University Press, 2006), 93 ff.

39 "This is a stickup!" Did robbers actually say this back in the day? Was it said only in the movies? Or was it invented for use on the radio, where the audience couldn't see what was happening?

In order to make clear that I'm speaking of more than the individuation of one-off actions, I'll adopt the term 'practical repertoire' from here on.

Framing

Our practical repertoire shapes our behavior; for as is well known in social psychology, the act-descriptions in which alternatives are framed strongly influence our choices.[40] Insofar as we choose among items in the socially shared repertoire, we are under the influence of a socially defined decision frame.

The framing effect is not just psychological but logical. In formal decision theory, acts are represented as choices of outcomes or of gambles on possible outcomes. The things that can be done — the doables — are determined by the outcomes that can be chosen or gambled on. Decision theorists have noted that what counts as rational or irrational, in the terms of their theory, depends on how doables are individuated.

John Broome illustrates this point with the example of an agent who seems to have irrational preferences because he prefers sightseeing over mountaineering, mountaineering over staying at home, and staying at home over sightseeing.[41] Broome explains that this agent's options can be subdivided according to the alternatives rejected, yielding options such as mountaineering-instead-of-sightseeing, mountaineering-instead-of-staying-home, and so on. The agent's preferences can then be represented as rational, since the act of mountaineering-instead-of-sightseeing may be dispreferred as unsophisticated, the act of staying-home-instead-of-mountaineering dispreferred as cowardly, and the act of sightseeing-instead-of-staying-home dispreferred as over-tiring, given that sophistication and courage are no longer at issue. Broome says that re-description may be appropriate in this case, because it draws distinctions that make a rational difference. As Broome points out, however, we can erase intransitivity in any set of preferences whatsoever by subdividing the options in this fashion, and decision theory cannot distinguish between the cases in which doing so

---

40   See, e.g., Amos Tversky and Daniel Kahneman, "The Framing of Decisions and the Psychology of Choice", *Science* 211, no. 4481 (1981): 453–458.

41   *Weighing Goods* (Oxford: Blackwell, 1991), Chapter 5. See also "Can a Humean Be Moderate?", in *Value, Welfare, and Morality*, ed. R.G. Frey and Christopher W. Morris (Cambridge: Cambridge University Press, 1992), 51–73, p. 58. For a discussion of this phenomenon, see my paper "The Story of Rational Action", *Philosophical Topics* 21, no. 1 (1993): 229–253; reprinted in *The Possibility of Practical Reason*.

is illuminating and those in which it amounts to sheer gerrymandering. Broome therefore argues that decision theory must be supplemented by "principles of rational indifference", which will rule out irrelevant distinctions among alternatives.

Yet principles of rational indifference will not help us decide whether to have the concepts of *mountaineering* and *sightseeing* to begin with. If people lack the concepts of mountaineering or sightseeing, they lack options for how to spend their spare time, and not for lack of mountains or sights. In order to do what we call sightseeing, they would first have to invent it.[42] And then there may be a rational difference, in Broome's sense, between mountaineering-instead-of-sightseeing and mountaineering in a context where sightseeing is not an alternative. Similarly, there may be a rational difference between truth-telling where *vranyo* is an alternative and truth-telling where it is not. Inventing an action-type therefore alters the decision frame, and even if there are principles of rational indifference for the resulting frame, there can be no rational principles for whether to invent a new action-type, since inventions are not chosen from among alternatives.

Foundations for Moral Relativism

Do Anglo-American readers of this book have a moral disagreement with people who practice *kala:m, étok-étok, kizb,* or *vranyo*? It would seem odd for us to condemn those practices as dishonest. The strongest negative attitude we are likely to have is to be glad that we don't live among the practitioners, while granting that if we did, we probably wouldn't regret it. Alternatively, we might feel somewhat envious of the Russians, whose social life is spiced with creative bluffing. In any case, none of these attitudes would support moral agreement or disagreement, despite our own moral seriousness in matters of truth-telling and candor.

---

42 Note that 'sightseeing' is not what moral philosophers call a thick concept, since it is evaluatively neutral. To offer someone a day of sightseeing is neither to recommend nor to disparage the option. Yet the presence of 'sightseeing' in our practical repertoire has some practical import simply in virtue of defining the option in the first place — in virtue, that is, of constituting it as a doable. The notion of thick descriptions was introduced by Gilbert Ryle, "The Thinking of Thoughts: What is 'Le Penseur' Doing?", reprinted in his *Collected Essays 1929–1968: Collected Papers Volume 2* (London: Hutchinson, 1971), 480–496. See also Clifford Geertz, "Thick Description: Toward an Interpretive Theory of Culture", Chapter 1 of *The Interpretation of Cultures* (New York: Basic Books, 1973), 1–31.

The fact is that each community has inherited from its ancestors a vast decision frame consisting in a distinctive taxonomy of actions. An inhabitant of one community can of course consider the option of relocating to another, but he can consider that option only under an act-description available within his own decision frame. There is no neutral act-description under which to choose a community: our *emigrating* may be no more universal an action-type than *mountaineering* or *sightseeing*.

The appearance of inter-community disagreement is often due to comparisons between action-types that are not in fact alternatives. If we Anglo-Americans deprecate *étok-étok* by saying, "They ought to tell the truth," we are using a concept of truth-telling that may not be rationally salient, or even available, in a community where *étok-étok* is a common form of indicative utterance. *Étok-étok* must be evaluated in the context of the speech acts available within the same decision frame.

In order to evaluate the practice of *étok-étok*, then, we would have to ask the Javanese why, in a particular situation, they choose *étok-étok* over some other speech act available to them, a question to which, according to Geertz, the answer would be, "You don't have to have a reason; you just *étok-étok*" — at which point we would realize that it's going to be a long night. The first answer or demurral will lead to another and another, until we have mapped out a very large web of practices and reasons, to which the only possible reaction will be relief or regret that we aren't Javanese.

The obstacle to disagreement is not that we cannot commensurate between conceptual schemes. Let us grant that the anthropologists have enabled us to understand the range of action-types available to the practitioners of *étok-étok*. The problem is that if we deprecate *étok-étok* as against the actual alternatives, we will be engaged in an intra-community disagreement — disagreeing as one Javanese with another — thereby conceding the point that disagreement must take place within a cultural context. And given the framing effect, there is a good chance that we will end up choosing to *étok-étok* after all.

IV. Foundations for Moral Relativism

I am not going to argue for moral relativism. The case for moral relativism is not an argument; it's a pair of observations. The first observation is that people live and have lived by mutually incompatible moral norms. The second observation is that no one has ever succeeded in showing any one set of norms to be universally valid.

These observations do not prove that there is no universally valid morality, but they do lead us to wonder: If there weren't a universally valid morality, would there be any valid morality at all? Could there be multiple moralities, each of merely local validity? To explain how there could be would be to lay foundations for moral relativism.

Formulating Relativism

According to moral relativism, saying that an action is wrong is like saying that someone is tall, a claim that is elliptical unless indexed to a reference class, since someone who is tall for an Mbuti may not be tall for a Kikuyu, and it makes no sense to ask whether he is tall *simpliciter*.[1] Similarly, says relativism, it makes no sense to ask whether an action or practice is wrong *simpliciter*. Claims of wrongness must be about wrongness-for-members-of-*x*, where *x* ranges over different cultures or societies or, as I will call them, communities.[2]

---

1 Yes, there may be a standard for human beings, tall for a human, which applies to all of us. But that standard is still relative to a reference class, namely, human beings. What's tall for a human is not tall for a giraffe. What's tall for a giraffe is not tall for a tree. The Milky Way is said to be 2,000 light years tall.

2 I will use the word 'community' to emphasize that I am speaking of people who regularly interact, usually because they live together. I will use the word 'social' as the corresponding adjective. I will speak as if communities are well defined and as if every individual belongs to one and only one community. Both of these assumptions are false but helpful as idealizations.

DOI: 10.11647/OBP.0029.04

The reason why it makes no sense to speak of tallness *simpliciter* is that there is no universal standard for who qualifies as tall. The standard applicable to the Kikuyu can't be applied to the Mbuti, nor to the Inuit or Uighur, either. Similarly, says relativism, there is no universal standard of what qualifies as wrong; the only standards that exist are restricted in application to particular communities.

This claim implies that when the Kikuyu say that there isn't anything wrong with female circumcision and the Mbuti say there is, both may be speaking the truth, because one group is speaking of what's wrong-for-the-Kikuyu while the other is speaking of what's wrong-for-the-Mbuti.[3] Of course, the Kikuyu and the Mbuti have a practical disagreement: they disagree over how to treat young women. According to moral relativism, however, there is no proposition whose truth is at issue between them.[4]

Moral relativism cannot rest with this negative conclusion, however. It must go on to claim that being wrong-for-the-Mbuti is a way of being morally wrong, just as being tall-for-an-Mbuti is a way of being physically tall. In other words, moral relativism must not only deny the existence of universal morality; it must also assert the existence of local moralities. Otherwise, it won't be relativism; it will just be nihilism.

The problem is that the relevant local institutions are *mores*, which seem to lack normative force.[5] "Female circumcision is permissible among the Kikuyu but not among the Mbuti" is the sort of statement found in academic ethnographies, which are fastidiously non-judgmental. An ethnographer might add that members of a community adhere to its *mores* from a desire for solidarity or a fear of sanctions, social or divine; but these additions would just pile on more ethnographic facts. They might also suggest instrumental reasons for community members to obey the local *mores*, given a desire for solidarity or a fear of sanctions. But moral relativism is

---

3 The proper term for this practice is a matter of controversy. I chose 'female circumcision' because it is widely used and somewhat value-neutral, though it is far from ideal. (Its evaluative force may depend on whether male circumcision becomes widely viewed as immoral.)

4 Some claim that there is a version of moral relativism according which the Kikuyu and Mbuti are disagreeing about a single proposition but faultlessly so, since both are right. I think that faultless disagreement is impossible, and so I ignore this version of relativism.

5 This objection is equivalent to one that is raised by Paul Boghossian. See his "What is Relativism?", in *Truth and Realism*, ed. Patrick Greenough and Michael P. Lynch (Oxford: Oxford University Press, 2006), 13–37, and "Three Kinds of Relativism", in *A Companion to Relativism*, ed. Steven D. Hales (Oxford: Wiley-Blackwell, 2011), 53–69.

not the view that the universal norm of instrumental reasoning leads to different conclusions under different circumstances.

A moral relativist must claim that the *mores* of a community can be fundamental, underived norms. The problem for the relativist is that *mores* and morality are as different as facts and values. How can relativism bridge that difference?

Perspectival Normativity

The difference can be bridged by the connection between facts and their action-guiding modes-of-presentation. 'A is wrong-for-members-of-*x*' is not the complete expression of a fact until the value of *x* is supplied; but it cannot guide action if that value is supplied explicitly. The value of *x* is explicitly supplied by anthropology textbooks, which name the community in question, thereby stating a normatively neutral fact. What members of the community say, however, is simply that A is wrong, a statement that is normatively valenced. The latter statement should be interpreted as containing an implicit indexical, as in 'wrong-for-us', the reference of 'us' being supplied by the context of utterance, so that the statement expresses the fact that A is wrong for members of that community, the same fact expressed by the former statement. But the latter statement is normatively valenced because the reference of 'us' is left to be supplied by the context. "Female circumcision is wrong", said by an Mbuti, is action-guiding; "Female circumcision is wrong for the Mbuti" is not.

The essential indexical

Here I rely on insights in John Perry's paper "The Problem of the Essential Indexical".[6] Let me illustrate Perry's thesis with a mundane example.

---

6 John Perry, "The Problem of the Essential Indexical," *Noûs* 13, no. 1 (1979): 3–21; reprinted in *The Problem of the Essential Indexical and Other Essays, Expanded Edition* (Stanford, CA: CSLI Publications, 2000). See also Perry's "Self-Notions", *Logos* (1990): 17–31, and "Myself and I", *Philosophie in Synthetischer Absicht*, ed. Marcelo Stamm (Stuttgart: Klett-Cotta, 1998), 83–103, also reprinted in *The Problem of the Essential Indexical*. James Dreier based a version of speaker relativism on Perry's "essential indexical" in "Internalism and Speaker Relativism", *Ethics* 101, no. 1 (1990): 6–26. His goal is to explain how statements applying normative terms such as 'good' can express the speaker's motives, so that speakers who agree on the facts can disagree about values. My goal is to explain how the facts in virtue of which reasons are action-guiding can fail to be action-guiding.

If I am walking down Fifth Avenue at noon on New Year's Day, 2020, and I ask someone the way to Washington Square, he will say "It's straight ahead". The proposition he expresses, fully spelled out, will be that Washington Square lies straight ahead of David Velleman at noon on 1/1/2020. But the intended role of his utterance will be to say that Washington Square is straight ahead of me then, irrespective of who I am or what day and time it is. Even if I think that it is 1920 and that I am Edith Wharton, I will not be misled by this statement, although it is actually about David Velleman in the twenty-first century. Whether it expresses a proposition about David Velleman or Edith Wharton doesn't matter for the purpose of guiding me to Washington Square.

What's more, the statement would cease to serve that purpose if it were rephrased so as to specify the time and person concerned. "Washington Square is straight ahead of David Velleman at noon on 1/1/2020" would not tell me how to get to Washington Square — not, that is, unless I knew that I was David Velleman and that it was noon on 1/1/2020, so that I could infer that Washington Square was straight ahead of me then, irrespective of the time and person concerned. Thus, practical guidance is, in Perry's phrase, essentially indexical, in the sense that its function depends not only on which proposition it expresses but also on how that proposition is determined by the context — specifically, on its being determined in the same way as the reference of indexical expressions such as 'I', 'you', 'here', and 'now'. Spelling out the proposition so as to eliminate the role of context defeats the purpose of practical guidance.[7]

Yet spelling out the proposition is necessary to specifying the relevant fact. The fact relevant to my search for Washington Square is that Washington Square lies straight ahead of David Velleman at noon on 1/1/2020. The fact that Washington Square once lay straight ahead of Edith Wharton is irrelevant. My guide's directions will state the former, relevant fact, but as we have seen, they must do so without explicitly distinguishing it from the irrelevant fact about Edith Wharton.

Normative guidance works the same way. The fact that female circumcision is permissible among the Kikuyu has, among the Kikuyu,

---

7   All of the above applies, by the way, to the predicate 'tall' when it is used to guide action. If you ask whether someone is tall because you want to know whether to put on flats or heels, it won't help to be told that the person is tall in comparison to someone who is five-foot-eight — unless, of course, you know that you are five-foot-eight, so that you can derive the action-guiding conclusion that the person is tall.

an action-guiding mode-of-presentation — namely, that the practice is permissible, or "permissible-for-us". Specifying the frame of reference, by saying that the practice is permissible for the Kikuyu, transforms it from the Kikuyu's norm into the ethnographer's report, hence from normative to factual. When the Kikuyu say that the practice is permissible and the Mbuti say that it is not, their statements are diametrically opposed, but they are diametrically opposed presentations of different facts, like "Straight ahead" and "Straight back" spoken to pedestrians headed in opposite directions.

The normativity of reasons

I am going to assume that morality obligates its subjects by being rationally binding on them — more specifically, by generating complete and compelling reasons for them to act, or to hold practical attitudes such as desires or intentions. On this assumption, whether different communities can have different moralities will depend on whether they can have differently constituted reasons. Can the same set of facts constitute reasons for members of different communities to adopt different actions or attitudes?

This question must be formulated carefully. It must be about complete reasons: sets of facts that militate for or against an action or attitude without any additional assumptions. And it must ask whether community membership can modify the force of such reasons without entering into their content or into the descriptions of the actions or attitudes involved. As a relativist, that is, I cannot be content to treat a subject's community membership as a circumstance that appears in the content of the reasons that apply to him. I cannot be content to say, for example, that *needing shelter and being an Mbuti* is a reason for building a lean-to, whereas *needing shelter and being a Kikuyu* is a reason for building a hut. Even in the context of Mbuti deliberations, being a homeless Kikuyu would qualify as a reason for building a hut, though of course that circumstance would never arise. Nor can I, as a relativist, be content to include the subject's community membership in conditional act-descriptions, such as *building a hut if one is Kikuyu* or *building a lean-to if one is Mbuti*. Even in Kikuyu deliberations, needing shelter qualifies as a reason for building a lean-to if one is Mbuti, though a Kikuyu would satisfy this act-description by default, without having to build anything. I must rather treat community membership as determining what qualifies as a reason for what. I must say that one and the same set of facts gives the Mbuti a complete reason to build a lean-to and gives the Kikuyu a complete reason to build a hut, thus militating in different directions for reasoners from different communities.

A relativist about reasons cannot also be an anti-reductionist about them. Anti-reductionism about reasons is the view that there is no explaining or analyzing the relation between reasons, on the one hand, and the actions or attitudes that they are reasons for, on the other.[8] According to anti-reductionism, we can say that reasons are considerations that count or weigh or militate in favor of such things, but we are then using the phrases 'count . . .' or 'weigh . . .' or 'militate in favor' in a sense that means no more than "be a reason for".

The reason why a relativist cannot be anti-reductionist is that he needs to explain how one and the same set of facts can count or weigh or militate in favor of different things in different communities. Asked how reasons can do such a thing, an anti-reductionist would have to say that there is no explaining how: they just do. Not a satisfactory reply. If relativism is to be more than this bare and implausible assertion, it had better explain how the counting or weighing or militating relation can be modified by the subject's community membership; and so it had better have something to say about the nature of that relation.

At the same time, the relativist had better not go so far as to say that different communities reason in accordance with different relations between reasons and what they are reasons for, as if communities use different methods of practical reasoning. Such methods of reasoning would be merely conventional — the deliberative *mores* of one's community — and so the problem of explaining the normative force of *mores* would recur at the level of practical reasoning. Why would one be obligated to reason by local methods? To avoid this question, the relativist must characterize a single relation that reasons always bear to what they are reasons for. His relativism must then consist in the claim that one and the same relation is sensitive to differences among communities. The unavoidable question is: How?

---

8   See, e.g., T.M. Scanlon, *What We Owe to Each Other* (Cambridge, MA: Harvard University Press, 1999), Chapter 1: "Reasons".

Frames of Reference

In order to answer this question, I will draw on the image of reasons as having weight, though unlike the anti-reductionist, I will use that image as a tool for analyzing the relation between reasons and that which they favor. Comparing the force of reasons to weight can be fruitful because both phenomena give application to the notion of frames of reference. If the same set of facts can have different normative force in different communities, the explanation will be that different communities have different frames of reference — or, more colloquially, different perspectives or points of view. And of course there are different gravitational frames of reference, in which massive objects are pulled in different directions with different weight. So let me develop this analogy, beginning with some obvious facts about gravitation.

Rocks are heavy; that is, they tend to fall; that is, to accelerate downwards. But 'downwards' is an indexical, and so 'Rocks are heavy' is implicitly indexical as well. Whereas it expresses a true proposition when spoken by someone standing on Earth, it expresses a false proposition when spoken by an astronaut in outer space. The true proposition expressed on Earth by this sentence is that rocks tend to accelerate toward the Earth.

Of course, 'Rocks tend to accelerate toward the Earth' is true when spoken by anyone, including astronauts in space. But saying "Rocks tend to accelerate toward Earth" provides no practical guidance to anyone — for example, to someone who is wondering whether to let go of a rock. Saying "Rocks tend to accelerate toward Earth" gives him practical guidance only if he knows that he is standing on Earth, precisely so that he can derive an indexical mode-of-presentation, such as 'Rocks are heavy' or 'Rocks tend to fall'. What would provide the most immediate practical guidance, however, is hefting the rock in his hand to feel its weight. Saying "Rocks tend to fall" is an action-guiding description of the force by which he would be guided directly in handling the rock.

In outer space, rocks are weightless, and there is no direction that counts as *down*. A rock can have weight only where there is a gravitational force that establishes some direction as *down*, which is the direction of falling, which is the direction in which the rock tends to accelerate. Which direction is *down* depends on the direction of gravitational force, which determines the direction in which rocks tend to fall.

What if reasons were like rocks? In that case, a consideration would have the weight of a reason only where there was a force that established a direction in which reasons militate. The force by which reasons militate in some direction is normativity. To the direction in which they militate, let us give the name 'to be adopted', since we can speak of both actions and attitudes as being adopted by a subject. Just as gravity determines what's *down*, by causing material objects to accelerate in that direction, so normativity would determine what is *to be adopted*, by guiding subjects in the direction of adopting actions and attitudes. Like a rock, then, a reason would exert its weight within a frame of reference established by some weight-conferring force.

Corresponding to the statement that rocks are heavy on Earth would be a statement that some fact F weighs in favor of some action or attitude A from some perspective P. Like the statement that rocks are heavy on Earth, the statement that F weighs in favor of A from P would have no guiding force. By the same token, saying to someone who occupies P that F weighs in favor of A, like saying to someone on Earth that rocks are heavy, would offer guidance by describing a force exerted by the weighty item. Finally, considering weighty reason F while occupying P would be like hefting a heavy rock while standing on Earth: it would be the most immediate form of guidance.

Alternatively, saying that fact F favors action or attitude A from perspective P would be like saying that Washington Square is straight ahead from the perspective of heading south on Fifth Avenue: no practical guidance. Saying to someone in P that F favors A would be like saying to someone headed south on Fifth Avenue that Washington Square is straight ahead: an action-guiding description. Getting someone in P to consider F would be like pointing a tourist straight ahead down Fifth Avenue: direct practical guidance.

But what plays the role of gravity in the case of reasons? And what plays the role of Earth? Or, in other words, what is normativity and what generates it? According to the analogy, normativity must be a force that is present wherever considerations have the weight of reasons, as gravity is present wherever things have physical weight. Where present, the force must establish a "direction" *to be adopted*, as gravity establishes the direction *down*. And *to be adopted* must be a direction in which normativity guides subjects, as *down* is the direction in which things are weighed by gravity.

If we can identify such a force, we will see how the normativity of reasons might vary between communities without being simply a matter of deliberative *mores*. Reasons will turn out to have, not just a role in a local method of reasoning, but a constant nature, as considerations that have weight in virtue of coming under a particular force, which establishes a frame of reference. Their nature will nevertheless be compatible with their favoring different actions or attitudes, or the same ones to different degrees, in different frames. The remaining task for relativism will then be to explain how different communities generate different rational frames of reference, as Earth and Mars generate different gravitational frames.

Note the order of constitution suggested by this analogy. The force of gravity does not draw things in a direction that is antecedently constituted as *down*; rather, a direction is constituted as *down* by the force of gravity, which guides things toward massive objects such as Earth. If the analogy between normativity and gravity holds, then we should not expect normativity to draw us in the direction of what is antecedently constituted as *to be adopted*; rather, what is *to be adopted* will be constituted by the force of normativity, which draws us toward — well, toward whatever plays the role of Earth in the practical realm. What plays the role of Earth, thus generating normativity, remains to be seen.

Being Ordinary

As a moral relativist, I expect normative gravity to emanate from *mores*, which establish an agent's social frame of reference, within which he finds reasons for acting and reacting. So what force do *mores* generate to guide actions and attitudes?

At this point, I must veer into the realm of speculative sociology, since the present question hangs on the nature of social *mores*. Before I take that turn, let me note that I have completed my outline of the form that a relativist metaethical theory should take. From here on, I will be proposing a specific content for one such metaethical theory. I find this theory compelling, but the reader may wish to regard it as no more than an illustration of how the above outline can be filled in.

A genealogy of *mores*

Human beings have a practical need and a psychological drive to live together with other people — not just in proximity to them but in personal interaction with them. Personal interactions require mutual interpretation: you cannot deal with others as persons without trying to understand their actions and attitudes, and to make yourself similarly understood. Your drive toward sociality therefore entails a drive toward mutual interpretation.

I speak of a drive toward sociality rather than a desire because this motive is inchoate and multiply specifiable. It can be described as a drive toward connection with other people, a drive to function as a person among other persons, indeed simply to *be* a person, insofar as sociality is essential to personhood or personhood is a social status. No matter how it is described, this drive requires you to engage in mutual interpretation. And your role in mutual interpretation requires not only interpreting but also being interpretable.

Whenever you interact with others, it's as if you are on the computer's end of a classic Turing Test, trying to gain and maintain recognition from the person on the other end of the line. In the Turing Test, the computer must avoid being relegated to the status of a machine; in real life, you must avoid being relegated to the status of mentally ill or deficient, or just too weird to bother with. No matter what in particular is at stake in a particular interaction, your eligibility for social interaction in general is also at stake: the interaction can always be broken off on the grounds that you are not a qualified interactant. In order for your qualifications to be acknowledged, you not only have to demonstrate an ability to interpret the other person; you also have to make yourself interpretable *as* a person.

Donald Davidson argued that in order to interpret other people, you have to narrow down the range of possible interpretations by assuming that they believe what is true and desire what is good by your lights.[9] Davidson thought that this charitable assumption would be necessary in principle, no matter how much evidence or time or intelligence was available to you. For purposes of speculative sociology, however, it suffices to say that you have to make such an assumption in practice, because you must interpret people on the fly. You need, as it were, a library of sub-routines for real-time interpretation of other people, and they need sub-routines for real-time interpretation of you, if you and they are to interact. That's why you and they need to exercise Davidsonian charity: the sub-routines most ready to hand are those drawn from the interpreter's own beliefs and desires.

---

9   See, e.g., 'Radical Interpretation', *Dialectica* 27 (1973): 314–328, reprinted in *Inquiries into Truth and Interpretation* (Oxford: Clarendon Press, 2001).

Because you need to be interpreted as well as to interpret, however, you need to exercise more than charity. Even as you extend charity to others by assuming that they believe and desire what you do, you must rise to their charity by satisfying their corresponding assumption, thus making yourself susceptible to their interpretation. They will try to understand you by assuming that you believe and desire as they do, and you must gratefully comply, so as to make yourself understood. They must do likewise, by gratefully satisfying your charitable assumption about them. The result is that you and they must converge on what to believe and desire. You needn't converge perfectly, but eccentricities must form no more than a thin albeit salient layer atop a deep fund of shared attitudes. Even eccentric attitudes must come from a fairly limited set of alternatives.[10]

As the sociologist Harvey Sacks put it, people have to be ordinary — not completely ordinary, of course, but ordinary to a very large extent.[11] Even if they want to be extraordinary, or out of the ordinary, there are more or less ordinary ways of doing so, beyond which they would strike others in their community as humanoid creatures of some unrecognizable kind. An idiosyncratic sense of humor still has to qualify as a sense of humor, and a disposition to laugh at manhole covers doesn't qualify. A unique sartorial style still has to qualify as a style, not an inability to dress oneself. One can coin new slang expressions, invent new dances, but only within limits.

Before people can be ordinary, however, there has to be such a thing as ordinariness: there have to be ways that people ordinarily think, feel, and act. That's where *mores* come in. People who need to interact with one another need to converge on ways of thinking, feeling, and acting that will suggest plausible first-pass interpretations of one another in their swiftly developing interactions. Their social *mores* are ways of thinking, feeling, and acting on which they converge.

---

10 When it comes to real life and real-time interpretation, the relevant interpreters are the people with whom you need to interact and by whom you therefore need to be recognized as an interactant. These people are your community, as I am using the term.

11 "On Doing 'Being Ordinary'", in *Structures of Social Action: Studies in Conversation Analysis*, ed. J. Maxwell Atkinson and John Heritage (Cambridge: Cambridge University Press, 1984), 413–439.

Convergence in attitudes

Where to converge? In the case of what to think, the salient point of convergence is determined by the facts, but points of convergence are less constrained in the case of how to feel. Within broad constraints imposed by human nature (as I will discuss shortly), people have a fair amount of leeway in their responses, and they still need to converge on recognizable kinds of responses to recognizable kinds of things in recognizable kinds of circumstances.

For example, you need for people in your social vicinity to be able to tell whether you're being serious, and just saying so won't help unless they can tell that you're being serious. So you need for there to be matters about which seriousness is the recognized default in your social vicinity — matters that are known by your interactants to be taken seriously by their interactants — so that the people with whom you interact can assume that you're serious about those matters. And then you had better be serious about them. Conversely, you need for there to be matters about which the recognized default is joking or teasing. Now, people will assume that you're serious about what you care about, and so it's helpful if there are things that people in your social vicinity know that people in their vicinity generally care about, and if you too care about those things but not about the things that are generally known to be laughing matters.

You need for people to be able to tell whether you're angry, and to tell without having to ask, just in case you are. So you need for there to be matters about which anger is the recognized default — matters that are generally known to be generally such as to make people angry. Conversely, you need for there to be matters about which the recognized default is non-acknowledgement.[12] People will assume that you're angry, for example, when you have been offended, and so it's helpful if there are ways of being treated that are generally known to give offense, and if you too feel offended when treated in those ways but not in others.

I cannot emphasize enough that these social necessities allow for exceptions. You can afford to care about things that are generally known to be laughing matters or to overlook things that are generally known to give offense, but you cannot afford to do so in general. The most affordable exceptions are ones that do not require on-the-spot interpretation — hobbies,

---

12   See Thomas Nagel, "Concealment and Exposure", *Philosophy & Public Affairs* 27, no. 1 (1998): 3–30.

for example. Taking bottle-caps seriously is unproblematic, especially because you can pursue that hobby in the privacy of your home or in the company of other bottle-cap fanciers. By and large, however, the things you take seriously have to be matters that are generally taken seriously and generally known to be such.

Similarly, there are times and places where you can afford to be deceptive, secretive, or inscrutable by preventing others from interpreting you correctly. But again, those occasions have to be rare exceptions, lest you fail the social Turing Test and end up as a non-person.

The Normativity of Reasons

Now, there is a view — and it has to be the relativist's view — that the only reasons to value something are features that it shares with other things that are valued, by oneself and by people in general. This was Mill's view,[13] and it is the view presupposed in our usual justification of attitudes. That is, we justify our attitudes by showing that they are ordinary, for ourselves and for those in our social vicinity.

Imagine (just imagine!) that we live in a community that admires people along lines of wealth. About a particular millionaire, we will say, "Now, *that's* the sort of person we admire," which is a way of saying that the person is admirable. Of course, one of us could point to rich people whom we don't admire and poor people whom we do, thereby initiating a discussion of whether rich people really are admirable, given that we don't ordinarily admire them. Alternatively, the dissenter may say, "That's the sort of person others admire, but I don't admire people like that." We can then ask what sort of people he does admire, what makes them desirable to him as role models or mentors, what he finds remarkable or estimable in them, and so on. If he points to things that we don't ordinarily desire in role models and mentors, or note and esteem in others, we can ask what he hopes to learn from such people or regrets lacking in comparison to them. And unless those questions, and the natural follow-up questions, eventually lead to attitudes that are somehow ordinary, his attempt at justification will fall flat.

---

13   In Chapter IV of *Utilitarianism*, in *On Liberty and Utilitarianism* (New York: Bantam Books, 1993). Often dismissed as a fallacious argument, it is rather a substantive claim.

Or perhaps one of us will say, "I think we all admire the wrong sort of person." This dissenter can then be asked what makes such people unremarkable and uninteresting, undesirable as role models or mentors, and so on; which will lead to questions such as what we ordinarily desire in role models and mentors, what we ordinarily take note of or an interest in, and so on; which may raise the objection that we desire the wrong sort of role model, for example; which may then lead to the question what about them is undesirable. But unless those questions, and natural follow-up questions, eventually lead to attitudes that are somehow ordinary, the dissenter's attempt at justification will fall flat.

Finally, a dissenter may say, "Hell, I just don't admire her." This dissenter can do without ordinariness, but at the cost of doing without justification.

Within our imaginary community, then, the fact that a person is rich constitutes a presumptive reason for admiring him, although the presumption in favor of its being a reason can be defeated in any of the ways that I have just surveyed, all of which appeal to presumptive reasons for desire or esteem or regret or some other attitude. Wealth is a presumptive reason for admiration in this community, I claim, because we have converged on admiring rich people so as to facilitate mutual interpretation with respect both to whom we admire and to how we regard the rich. The normative force of this reason is the force of the drive toward mutual interpretability, which arises out of the drive toward sociality.

One might think: The fact that some people are ordinarily admired is merely evidence that they are admirable; it isn't what makes them admirable. I say: Then why do communities converge within themselves but diverge from one another with respect to whom they admire? Can we residents of Greenwich Village assert categorically that widely cited scholars are admirable but widely viewed televangelists are not? Or must we rather conclude that there is no reason to admire one person more than another, hence no reason to admire anyone? Relativism offers a more plausible account of the phenomena. According to relativism, we residents of Greenwich Village have reason to admire Hannah Arendt and Elizabeth Anscombe, namely, that they were widely cited scholars; and their being so is a reason to admire them because that's the sort of people we admire.

One might think: The fact that we ordinarily admire scholars is no reason to admire them. I say: Right. Our admiring scholars isn't a reason to admire them; it's the frame of reference within which scholarship is a reason to admire them — a reason, specifically, for each of us. Compare: There cannot

IV. Foundations for Moral Relativism 59

be directions to Washington Square except from some perspective, but the perspective doesn't add to the directions. "Straight ahead" gives the directions; "Heading south on Fifth Avenue" gives the perspective. "Straight ahead for someone heading south on Fifth Avenue" doesn't give more complete directions; it gives no directions at all. "Straight ahead" gives complete directions. So too, "She's a widely cited scholar" gives a complete reason: information about our community membership would not add but would rather detract.

Compare again: Someone's being ordinarily admired has no weight from our perspective, no more weight than the Earth has on Earth. What plays the role of Earth in our evaluative universe is personal interaction with co-members of our community, which is made possible by mutual interpretability, which is made possible by convergence on ordinary attitudes. The community's evaluative frame of reference is established by the drive toward sociality plus the shared ways of thinking, feeling, and acting to which members of the community are thereby drawn. Other communities have their own evaluative frames of reference, established by the same force drawing them toward other ways of thinking, feeling, and acting, whichever are theirs. Hence reasons are relative to a community — specifically, to the community's *mores*, or shared way of life. In one community, scholarship is admirable; in others, not.

One might think: The drive that constitutes the force of reasons should be the drive toward doing what ought to be done and feeling what ought to be felt, not a drive toward some arbitrary aim like mutual interpretability. I say: Mutual interpretability is not an arbitrary aim in relation to the force of reasons. Actions and reactions are interpreted in light of reasons for adopting them. Whatever force makes one responsive to reasons makes one responsive to the very considerations that figure in interpretation.

One might think: Okay, but considerations figure in interpretation because they are reasons, not vice versa. I say: Yes, vice versa; that's the best account of the phenomena. On the one hand, we find genuine reasons for admiration; on the other, we find individually convergent and mutually divergent communities of admirers. The best explanation for these phenomena is that there is no such thing as what categorically ought to be admired; there are only reasons that acquire their weight from some perspective-establishing force, which cannot be the force of what categorically ought to be admired. That force is whatever force gives weight to reasons in general, everywhere. Our practices of justification, and their connection to interpretation, suggest that it is the drive to converge with our community on what to feel, which in turn is best explained by our drive toward mutual interpretability as a prerequisite of sociality.

One might think: This theory purports to reduce an 'ought' to an 'is', or a value to a fact, which we all know is impossible. The value is that scholars are admirable; the fact is that scholarship draws admiration from residents of Greenwich Village, who ordinarily admire scholars. The one cannot be reduced to the other. I say: Of course the value can't be reduced to that fact; what it can be — and has to be, given the nature of normativity — is an indexical mode-of-presentation of the fact. That scholars are admirable (that is, to us) is a normative, hence indexical, expression of the non-normative fact that scholarship draws admiration from residents of Greenwich Village.

Reasons for acting

Thus far, I have spoken of reasons for attitudes, which I have treated as the basis of values such as admirability, desirability, and so on. Morality involves not only reasons for attitudes but reasons for actions. I can be brief in presenting relativism about reasons for actions, since much of the work has already been done.

Reasons for attitudes acquire their normative force, I have said, from the drive toward mutual interpretability for the sake of sociality. If reasons for acting are to exert normative force, they should acquire it from the same drive in a similar way. The question, then, is what would make for mutual interpretability of behavior.

Interpretation is holistic. That is, an interpreter tries to figure out all at once what a subject is feeling, believing, and doing, and he tries to figure it out by looking for the suite of attitude- and act-descriptions that best fits the subject's present and past behavior overall. In order for the subject to make himself interpretable in real time, he must therefore behave in a way that clearly suggests some overall suite as the best fit. And what lies most within his control is of course his behavior, which he can fashion so as to fit his attitudes — or, preferably, those attitudes which he can most readily be interpreted as having.[14] As a rule, then, the subject's reasons for acting

---

14 These may not be attitudes that the subject actually has. I discuss this issue in "From Self-Psychology to Moral Philosophy", *Philosophical Perspectives 14: Action and Freedom* (2000): 349–377; reprinted in *Self to Self: Selected Essays* (New York: Cambridge University Press, 2005), 224–252.

will consist in his attitudes, especially those attitudes which he and others ordinarily have.[15]

This rule has many exceptions, however, as is inevitable whenever holistic reasoning is at work. For example, co-members of a community may coordinate on behaving in a particular way under particular circumstances no matter what they think or feel. They will then be able to read the applicable act-descriptions directly off the circumstances, because they will know what "we" do in circumstances of that kind. If they want to interpret the behavior in terms of the attitudes behind it, they will interpret it, not as an expression of attitudes peculiar to the agent at the time, but as conformity to a social convention for the sake of sociality, and they will find departures from the convention intelligible only if they can understand why the agent would have strong motives for departing from it.

And then there will be cases in which a subject has strong motives for being uninterpretable to co-members of his community — that is, for lying or keeping secrets or simply being inscrutable. Despite his drive toward interpretability to co-members of the community, such motives will give the subject reason for being in some respect uninterpretable them, lest he become uninterpretable to the minimal community consisting of himself.[16] The subject himself is, as it were, the core of his own normative Earth.

---

15 Some will object that reasons for acting are not attitudes but their contents or the satisfiers thereof. They will say that reasons for adding sage to a stew, for example, include the desirability of improving the taste and the fact that sage will improve it, not the desire to improve the taste or the belief that sage will do so. I am not sure whether Donald Davidson, the author of this example, disagrees. He thinks that the desire and belief are the *reasons for which* the agent adds sage to the stew, but he also thinks that 'It is desirable to improve the taste' and 'It will improve the taste' are the premises in the agent's practical reasoning, and he doesn't say whether the premises in practical reasoning are the relevant *reasons for* acting, as opposed to the *reasons for which* the agent acts. ("Intending", in *Essays on Actions and Events* [Oxford: Clarendon Press, 1980], 86.) I believe that *reasons for* doing something have to be such as could become the *reasons for which* someone does it, hence that there can be no distinction. (See Bernard Williams, "Internal and External Reasons", in *Moral Luck* [Cambridge: Cambridge University Press, 1982], 101–113.) I also believe that reasons in both cases are attitudes, not their contents or satisfiers, but I cannot defend that view here. See my *Practical Reflection* (Princeton, NJ: Princeton University Press, 1989) and *How We Get Along* (New York: Cambridge University Press, 2009).

16 This claim and the associated theory of agency are defended in my *Practical Reflection* (Princeton, NJ: Princeton University Press, 1989), some essays in *The Possibility of Practical Reason* (Ann Arbor, MI: MPublishing, 2009), some essays in *Self to Self*

Implications

My account thus far has the following implications. The Kikuyu may have reasons for practicing female circumcision, and if they have such reasons, they have them because they live like Kikuyu. Westerners have reason to abominate the practice, and they have those reasons because they live like Westerners.

One might wonder: "Perspectives aside, whose reasons are the real reasons?" I say: That's a nonsensical question, like asking "Perspectives aside, which are the correct directions to Washington Square?" or "Frames-of-reference aside, how heavy is this rock?" One might conclude: "Well, then, there are no real reasons, only reasons-from-a-perspective." I say: That's the wrong conclusion. From within a perspective, some facts really and truly have the normative force of reasons, just as from within a perspective, some utterances are really and truly the directions to Washington Square. Indeed — and this is the fundamental point — there is no other kind of normative force for reasons to have. Perspective-independent reasons are impossible, just like perspective-independent directions, because reasons and directions are action-guiding, and guidance is necessarily relative to a perspective.

Of course, the Kikuyu may actually have reasons within their own perspective to abolish the practice of female circumcision. The practice may be in violation of other Kikuyu *mores*, which generate reasons to abolish it. In that case, we can say, as a matter of anthropological fact, that the Kikuyu have reason to abolish the practice, and we can say to them, "You have reason to abolish that practice", while directing their attention to the considerations that might guide them to abolish it. Even without knowing whether the Kikuyu way of life generates such reasons, we may feel optimistic that it must, and we can engage them in conversation with the hope of discovering that it does. Relativism doesn't counsel despair over the possibility of moral coordination among communities.

What relativism does counsel, however, is humility. We cannot assume that the Kikuyu have reason to change their ways. We have to allow for the possibility that at the end of the conversation, common ground will still be out of reach.

(New York: Cambridge University Press, 2005), and *How We Get Along* (New York: Cambridge University Press, 2009).

Is This Really Relativism?

By now, the reader may wonder whether I am really a relativist. And indeed there are several respects in which my view departs from the extreme and simplistic relativism that is usually associated with the name.

Universality vs. ubiquity

One reason for doubting whether I am a relativist is that I seem to have allowed my evaluative universe to fall under universal purposes and principles — first the aim of mutual interpretability and then the various rules that subserve it, such as Davidsonian charity and (as I call it) generosity. How can a relativist allow such norms to govern universally?

In fact, I haven't granted universality to any norms. As Sharon Street has pointed out, a norm needn't hold universally in order to hold within every perspective, since it can hold independently within each one.[17] I will express this point by saying that a norm can be ubiquitous but not universal. Ubiquitous norms govern only locally, but they govern locally everywhere, within every perspective. An example is the taboo against incest. Some people point to the incest taboo as a "human universal", but they don't usually mean "universal" in the metaethical sense, since they don't think that there is a perspective-independent moral requirement that would be violated by a community that permitted incest. In the metaethical sense, then, they regard the taboo as ubiquitous but not universal.

A moral relativist had better deny the existence of any universal norms, moral or otherwise; for if he concedes the existence of universal norms, he will be hard-pressed to explain why moral norms are not among them.[18] But a moral relativist must go further. Although there being no universal norms would entail that moral norms are at most ubiquitous, they might still be ubiquitous in a way that the moral relativist must also deny; for even if moral norms were merely ubiquitous, they might be necessarily so. The principles of charity and generosity, for example, are necessarily ubiquitous norms, in the sense that they are operative independently in every normative frame of reference. The fact that these principles are

---

17   See Street's "Objectivity and Truth: You'd Better Rethink It" (forthcoming) and "How to Be a Relativist About Normativity" (in progress).

18   A similar point is made by Paul Boghossian in "Three Kinds of Relativism" and by Street in "How to Be a Relativist About Normativity". Note that I am speaking here of *practical* norms; epistemic norms are a different matter.

locally operative everywhere is no accident: each normative frame of reference must be established by the drive of its occupants toward sociality, which requires mutual interpretability, which calls for charity on their part as interpreters and generosity on their part as targets of interpretation.[19] Where this force is absent, there are no reasons for acting or reacting, and no actions or attitudes are *to be adopted*: everything is normatively weightless.

As a believer in the necessary ubiquity of these principles, I am not a relativist about Davidsonian charity or generosity. I am a moral relativist, however, because I deny that any moral norms have the same status as those principles. In sum, I deny that there are universal norms of any kind, and that there are necessarily ubiquitous norms of morality.

Plural moralities

Another reason for doubting my credentials as a relativist is my assumption that the *mores* of actual communities will not diverge so far from ours as to be utterly a-moral by our lights. I assume that the *mores* of actual communities always have enough in common with our morality to be recognizable to us as versions — often misguided versions, even horrifically or appallingly misguided versions, but still recognizably versions — of what we call morality.

Why so? If there is no single true morality but many moralities, then why aren't there communities with no morality at all, because their *mores* are utterly a-moral?

The beginning of an answer is that members of a community cannot achieve mutual interpretability by converging on just any attitudes and actions. The eligible points of convergence are constrained by human nature. There are some attitudes on which we humans cannot help but converge. They include an aversion to pain, separation, and frustration; an inclination toward pleasure, connection, and the fluid exercise of skill; the inborn and automatic fight-or-flight response; an interest in the human face and form; an initial dislike of snakes, spiders, blood, and the dark; plus an array of physiological appetites. Human nature also gives every attitude a distinctive role in causing behavior. Admiration (to stick with my example) naturally disposes one to emulate the admired person, to defer to him, and to approve of his words and actions. These behaviors may be more or less readily

---

19 Norms can be necessarily ubiquitous for other reasons. See, again, Street's "How to Be a Relativist About Normativity".

interpretable in light of one's other attitudes. One may have beliefs that harmonize or clash with the person's opinions; ideals that he may or may not exemplify; interests that he may or may not share; likes and dislikes of other people whom he may resemble. Now consider a category of people who tend to have opinions we ordinarily reject, interests we ordinarily disdain, resemblances to people we ordinarily hate. Converging on admiration for such people will not serve the purpose of mutual interpretability. We will rather tend to converge on admiring people admiration for whom makes us more readily interpretable, because admiration for them harmonizes with other attitudes on which we converge. And we will tend to converge on types of action that are readily interpretable in light of such attitudes

There is reason to think that the resulting constellation of attitudes and actions will tend to be pro-social rather than anti-social, in the sense that they will favor mutual benefit over mutual harm. The reason is that our convergence must result from spontaneous, unmanaged coordination, which favors mutually beneficial arrangements.

Hume illustrates this point with the example of two people rowing a boat together.[20] If these people were riding a tandem bicycle instead, then each would be tempted to ease off the pedals and let the other do most of the work. (Maybe that's why tandem bicycles are used for leisurely sightseeing but not for travelling from point A to point B.) But if two people are travelling by rowboat and each is pulling one of the oars, then trying to shift the workload will be self-defeating, since the boat will go around in circles.[21] In order to go anywhere, the rowers need to produce equal work: they need to coordinate on a level of effort. Fortunately, the rowers can coordinate spontaneously, without exchanging a word, provided that there is a uniquely salient level on which to converge, as there will be if some point of convergence is obviously preferred by both. Each rower prefers a level high enough to get them where they are going but not so high as to wear them out; if some such level is obvious, then they will spontaneously coordinate on it. The need to coordinate thus produces mutually beneficial joint effort.

---

20 *A Treatise of Human Nature*, ed. L.A. Selby-Bigge, with text revised and notes by P.H. Nidditch (Oxford: Clarendon Press, 1976), III.ii.2, 490.

21 David Lewis assumes that the rowers must synchronize their strokes (*Convention: A Philosophical Study* [Cambridge, MA: Harvard University Press, 1969], 44 *et passim*). In fact, the rowers need not synchronize their strokes, so long as their oars do equal amounts of work.

Or consider two people who are trying to move a sofa by picking it up at either end. If they were hoisting the sofa with a block and tackle, each would be tempted to slack off and let the other do the pulling, but straight lifting requires them to lift their ends equally fast and equally high. The need to coordinate will lead them to converge on that degree of force, if there is one, that is uniquely salient as the one on which to converge; the most salient degree will be the one, if there is one, that is obviously preferred by both; and the obviously preferable degree will the one, if there is one, that will get the job done without straining anyone's back. If there is such a degree of force, then the movers will converge on it, and the result, again, will be mutually beneficial joint effort.[22]

For the same reason, what becomes ordinary in a community — the constellation of feelings and actions on which its members converge — is likely to favor mutual benefit over harm. Different communities, already made alike by human nature, will also be shaped alike by the need for coordination, which favors their pro-social over their anti-social human tendencies. The variance among social *mores* will therefore resemble the variance among variations on a theme, where the theme is recognizably moral.

So although I believe that there is no necessarily ubiquitous morality, I also believe that having a recognizably moral way of life is indeed necessarily ubiquitous. The difference between our community and others is not that we have a morality and they have none; the difference is that their ways of life and ours embody common moral themes in incompatible ways. And the fact that all ways of life embody those themes is no accident. Shared ways of life arise from the need for mutual interpretability, which requires co-ordination, which favors mutually beneficial arrangements; and so ways of life, by their very nature, tend to be recognizably moral, however horrifically or appallingly so.

---

22   Another example, further afield: What is the rationale for social sanctions against nonconformists? The rationale is not that nonconformity itself is harmful to society, nor that most people just happen to behave pro-socially, so that the sanctions happen to fall on the anti-social. The rationale is that the sanctions themselves militate in favor of pro-social behavior, by enforcing coordination. Given common knowledge that everyone will be penalized for being an exception, people will tend to converge on what they prefer to be the rule, and they prefer a rule of pro-social behavior to the alternatives. Thus, the point of sanctioning nonconformists is not that the nonconformists harm the group; the point is that the sanctions themselves benefit the group, by introducing an incentive for coordination, which favors mutually beneficial behavior.

The possibility of progress

Here is yet a third respect in which my version of relativism may seem un-relativistic. According to my version, the fact that reasons are always relative to a perspective does not entail that perspectives themselves are on a par. Even if people do have reason for practicing female circumcision, I say, the possibility remains that those reasons depend on perspectives that are backwards, and not just from a particular perspective.

My fellow relativists will be shocked by the suggestion that one community can be less advanced than another, and not just from someone's perspective. Nothing could be further from the spirit of relativism. But as I said at the outset, a relativist has to characterize a single relation that reasons bear to actions or practical attitudes, lest he end up with deliberative *mores* whose normativity needs to be explained. The guiding force mediated by that relation will be a single normative force, the same force in every perspective, perspective-dependent only as to its direction. Such a force will unavoidably provide a necessarily ubiquitous parameter in relation to which ways of life can be more or less advanced.

I say that the necessarily ubiquitous parameter is mutual interpretability, which is a prerequisite for social life. The standard of comparison for practical perspectives is thus the degree to which they facilitate mutual interpretability. How well have members of a community managed to converge on reasons for acting and reacting? How well do those reasons help them to understand themselves as the kind of creatures they are, endowed with a somewhat fixed nature as human beings? How well, in other words, have the members of a community managed to develop a shared way of human life?

The idea is that there is something that ways of life characteristically *do*.[23] Members of a community, any community, develop a way of life for the sake of its doing that thing. Some ways of life do it better than others. Those ways of life are more advanced with respect to an aim shared by all communities in developing their ways of life. Those ways of life are more advanced, in other words, with respect to a necessarily ubiquitous social aim.

---

23 There is much in common between this functionalist view and the "pluralistic relativism" of David Wong in *Natural Moralities: A Defense of Pluralistic Relativism* (Oxford: Oxford University Press, 2006), esp. Chapter 2.

What's left

At this point, my fellow relativists may want to banish me from their midst. My so-called relativism, they will say, is no relativism at all, because it allows for evaluative distinctions among ways of life. What is left of relativism in my view?

For one thing, the evaluative distinctions that remain are not moral. Communities do not qualify as more or less advanced by falling closer or further from some universal or ubiquitous morality. There is no universal or even ubiquitous morality, and there are no universal norms of any kind. What there are, however, are ubiquitous norms of interpretation and interpretability, which are the fundamental prerequisites of sociality, and it is in relation to these norms that communities can be more or less advanced. They can be more or less advanced, in other words, in terms of the prerequisites of sociality.

Secondly, my view says that reasons for actions and attitudes are relative to the way of life that actually prevails in an agent's actual community. We Westerners are therefore in no position to say that a Kikuyu mother has reason not to circumcise her daughter — unless, that is, we can locate such reasons within the Kikuyu way of life. Even if our Western way of life is more advanced, it cannot provide reasons to the members of communities who follow different ways.

Thirdly, even if the Kikuyu community as a whole can have reasons for revising its way of life, those reasons will be relative to the way of life it already has, and there are no grounds for assuming that they will lead it to converge with other communities. If a whole community is to have reasons to change, those reasons must consist in circumstances in light of which social change would be interpretable, at least to members of that community, and what's interpretable by way of change in a community depends on what the community is already like. Reason-guided change is path-dependent: where it ends up depends on where it began. So different communities may have reason to change in ways that still lead to different ways of life, even if those ways of life are equally advanced by necessarily ubiquitous standards.[24]

---

24 Revolutionary change is another matter. I discuss this issue in "Motivation by Ideal", *Philosophical Explorations* 5, no. 2 (2002): 89–103; reprinted in *Self to Self*.

There may some day be world-wide convergence, if there is a world-wide community — the proverbial global village — but even then, relativism would hold. If as a result of advances in transportation and communication, everyone has to be prepared to interact with just about anyone, then a global way of life may develop, and cultural diversity will vanish. But which way of life became global would still be path-dependent, and what people had reason for feeling and doing would still be relative to the way of life in which mankind happened to end up, given where it began.

Moral Debate

Finally, a warning to philosophers. We cannot eyeball various communities and see how well their ways of life facilitate mutual intelligibility. Differences in success between ways of life are usually too subtle to discern from an academic perspective, least of all from the philosopher's study. We just have to inhabit a particular way of life and do the daily work of interpreting, being interpretable, and helping to develop a common ground that facilitates mutual interpretation. Progress comes from a collective experiment in living, and there is no substitute for participating in the experiment.

So there is no point in appealing to an explicit standard of progress when engaging in philosophical debate or in face-to-face disagreement with members of other communities. The rational way to disagree with those who live differently is to articulate our own self-understanding, listen as they articulate theirs, and then go back to our respective experiments to see whether we have learned something by which to understand ourselves better by living differently. We can thereby make progress of a sort that cannot be detected or directed from without.

The reason for talking with those who live differently is that we and they share at least some common ground, since all of us are trying to figure out how to make better sense of and to ourselves as human beings. We even have reason to think that conversation will lead to progress. Indeed, we have reason to think that it will lead to progress that is recognizably moral, because our need for mutual intelligibility has its source in our sociality.

V. Sociality and Solitude[1]

The moral universe of relativism is a scary place. Bad enough that there are physical black holes; relativism raises the specter of moral black holes as well, places where the laws of morality collapse. The fear is not just that there can be ways of life in which this or that unsavory practice turns out to be morally permissible; it's that there can be ways of life that draw no distinctions remotely like our distinction between right and wrong, so that nothing is either permissible or impermissible in a sense that we can recognize as moral.

Lucky for us, the nearest physical black hole is 1,600 light-years away — nearby on a cosmic scale but far enough away for us to sleep at night. What would it take to reassure us likewise about moral black holes? Realists and rationalists have the comfort of believing that moral black holes are impossible: wherever there are people, they believe, recognizably moral norms are in force. But what comfort is there for those of us who are relativists? We must look for comfort in the possibility that moral black holes are very far away, not in physical space, of course, but in moral space, the space occupied by possible ways of life.

For this kind of reassurance, empirically minded moral philosophers typically look to natural selection as favoring the development of moral motives such as sympathy and altruism, or an instinctive sense of fairness. The reason for this emphasis, I think, is once again the sense of moral danger, the sense that there might never have been a distinction between what's right-ish and what's wrong-ish, much less between right and wrong. Realists and rationalists try to rule out this possibility in advance, but others

---

1 Ralph Waldo Emerson wrote an essay with the title "Society and Solitude" (*Society and Solitude: Twelve Essays* [Cambridge, MA: The Riverside Press, 1870]). I wish it were relevant.

DOI: 10.11647/OBP.0029.05

must admit it, and then they find the force of natural selection tempting as a replacement for *a priori* necessity.

I have nothing against sympathy and altruism, but like Kant, I believe that morality has more to do with valuing the personhood of people than with promoting their interests or feeling their pain. I also side with Kant in believing that personhood consists in rational nature; I'll have something to say in a moment about the aspects of rational nature in which I believe personhood to consist. Unlike Kant, however, I think that valuing personhood is rooted in human nature, not in requirements of pure practical reason. My aim in this chapter is to give an *a posteriori* account of some ways in which personhood is naturally valued by human beings.

Objective Self-Awareness

Our response to personhood is expressed by Thomas Nagel, reflecting on personhood in himself. Nagel asks,[2]

> [H]ow can I be merely a particular person? The problem here is not how it can be the case that I am this one rather than that one, but how I can be anything as specific as a particular person in the world — any person.

> How can I be anything so small and concrete and specific?
> I know this sounds like metaphysical megalomania of an unusually shameless kind. Merely being TN isn't good enough for me: I have to think of myself as the world soul in humble disguise. In mitigation I can plead only that the same thought is available to any of you.[3]

To some, Nagel may sound disappointed with his personhood. To my ear, however, he is expressing a sense of wonder, albeit wonder at finding himself to be a wonderfully humble phenomenon.

---

2   "The Objective Self", in *Knowledge and Mind: Philosophical Essays*, ed. Carl Ginet and Sydney Shoemaker (New York: Oxford University Press, 1983), 212. See also "Subjective and Objective", in *Mortal Questions* (Cambridge: Cambridge University Press, 1979), 196–213; "The Limits of Objectivity", in *The Tanner Lectures on Human Values*, Vol. I, ed. Sterling M. McMurrin (Salt Lake City: University of Utah Press, 1980), 77–139; and *The View From Nowhere* (New York: Oxford University Press, 1986), Chapter IV. *The View From Nowhere* is perhaps the most widely read of these works, but its chapter on "the objective self" is, in my view, considerably watered down. I recommend the paper entitled "The Objective Self" in the volume edited by Ginet and Shoemaker.

3   Nagel, "The Objective Self", 225.

Why is Nagel amazed at being anything so concrete and specific as a particular person? Did he think he was a universal? There must be something he felt himself to be, in contrast to which his concrete specificity amazes him.

Before dealing directly with these quotations from Nagel, I will have to discuss a feature of personhood that they express, namely, a person's objective self-conception. The self-conception that Nagel expresses is not just the subjective, egocentric conception of the world from the perspective of an unrepresented 'I'; it's the conception of himself as a creature with this very conception of itself. This self-conception is objective in the sense that it represents its subject *as* its subject in the world — a member of the objective order, standing in an objective relation to this very thought.[4]

An objective self-conception is distinctive of persons and, I believe, constitutive of their personhood.[5] My basis for saying that it is constitutive of personhood is functionalist. If you want to know what it is to be a person, I say, look for ways in which it is characteristic of persons to function, and then look for what those functions have in common. What is common to the characteristic functions of persons, I will argue, is that they require and manifest an objective self-conception. I will not survey an exhaustive list of the functions that are characteristic of persons, but I will cover many functions that only and almost all persons perform: making plans that resolve an open future; participating in conversation and in joint intentions; and enjoying distinctively personal modes of togetherness and apartness — that is, of sociality and solitude.

Many of the functions that I discuss will turn out to be functions for which we value persons. What we are thereby committed to valuing,

---

4 Exactly how there can be such a self-conception is a vexed question, which, fortunately, needn't be answered here. Especially fortunate is that forms of reflexive thought have been extensively explored by John Perry. See his "Self-Notions", *Logos* (1990): 17–31, and "Myself and 'I'", in *Philosophie in Synthetischer Absicht*, ed. Marcelo Stamm (Stuttgart: Klett-Cotta, 1998), 83–103. See also "The Problem of the Essential Indexical", *Noûs* 13, no. 1 (1979): 3–21. The last two pieces are reprinted in *The Problem of the Essential Indexical and Other Essays, Expanded Edition* (Stanford, CA: CSLI Publications, 2000). Note that whereas Perry focuses on the reflexive thought by which a person thinks of himself, I focus on that by which a person also thinks of this very reflexive thought. The phenomena of interest to me involve thoughts that are self-referring in the sense that they refer not only to their subjects but also to themselves.

5 I think it is possible that some of the higher apes have an objective self-conception. If they do, then they are persons, in my view. This consequence of my view does not strike me as a counterexample, since I think that some of the higher apes just might be persons.

I will argue, is the capacity that makes those functions possible, namely, the capacity of persons to think of themselves as inhabitants of the world, thinking this thought.

Plans

I'll start with the role of an objective self-conception in plans. Plans are central to our agency, which is in turn central to our personhood. Michael Bratman puts the point like this:[6]

> The central fact is that we are planning agents. We frequently settle in advance on more or less complex plans concerning the future, and then these plans guide our later conduct. So much, anyway, is included in our commonsense understanding of the sort of beings we are. As planning agents, we have two central capacities. We have the capacity to act purposively; and we have the capacity to form and execute plans. The latter capacity clearly requires the former; but it is plausible to suppose that the former could exist without the latter. Indeed, it is natural to see many nonhuman animals as having only the former capacity and to see our possession of both capacities as a central feature of the sort of beings we are.

Like Bratman, I believe that planning is central to the sort of beings we are; I also claim that an objective self-conception is central to planning.

Some philosophers of action believe that plans have as their objects actions without agents, as expressed in the infinitive or gerundive of the verb. The attitude of planning to hang a picture, they believe, has as its object 'to hang a picture' or 'hanging a picture'. Yet I may plan, not to hang the picture, but rather that the picture be hung, or that we hang it together, and all of these plans seem to share a deep structure despite their differences at the surface. In order to support all of them, this structure must have an argument place for the intended agent or agents, who may or may not be mentioned when the plans are expressed. What gets expressed as the plan that the picture be hung is fundamentally a plan that someone or other hang it; what gets expressed as the plan to hang the picture with you is a plan that you and I hang it together; and so what gets expressed as the plan simply to hang the picture must be a plan that I hang it. In each case, there is some determination, implicit or explicit, as to the agent of the intended act.

---

6   *Intention, Plans, and Practical Reason* (Cambridge, MA: Harvard University Press, 1987), 2.

The attitude of planning to hang a picture thus includes a conception of myself as someone by whom a picture can be hung, just as it might be hung by someone else, either with me or alone. Indeed, it has to include a conception of myself as hanging the picture because of having hereby planned to hang it, not because I was already going to hang it anyway. I have to plan my own actions from the first-person perspective, but I simultaneously have to conceive of myself as an efficacious inhabitant of the objective world, and I have to conceive of my plan as itself efficacious in prompting or guiding me to act.[7]

This feature of plans accounts for the openness of the future from the planner's point of view.[8] 'That I hang a picture' is potentially a fact about the future, whereas 'to hang a picture' and 'hanging a picture' are not. When I plan to hang a picture, I represent what is going to come true as a result of my plan: I am going to hang a picture, because of having hereby planned to. If I planned instead to sell the picture, then I would represent something else as coming true as a result of my so representing it. I can therefore represent different ways the future will go, and in most cases, it will go that way, and for the very reason I have represented, namely, that I represented it that way. With respect to myself and the picture, then, there is no single way that I must represent the future in order to represent it correctly. From my planning perspective, the future is open: it will go however I think it will.

The Turing Test

Our need for an objective self-conception is suggested by the work of computer scientists following in the footsteps of Alan Turing.[9] Turing's eponymous test is a measure of a computer's ability to simulate a person. Computer scientists since Turing have discovered that in order for a computer to be recognized as a person, it must present a coherent persona, and so it must have a third-personal model of the person it is simulating.[10]

---

7   See Gilbert Harman, "Practical Reasoning", *The Review of Metaphysics* 79, no. 3 (1976): 440–448; and *Change in View: Principles of Reasoning* (Cambridge, MA: The MIT Press, 1986), Chapter 8.

8   Of course, plans do not make the future metaphysically open; they make it only epistemically open. I discuss this phenomenon in "Epistemic Freedom", *Pacific Philosophical Quarterly* 70, no. 1 (1989): 73–97; reprinted in *The Possibility of Practical Reason* (Ann Arbor, MI: MPublishing, 2000), 32–55.

9   Alan Turing, "Computing Machinery and Intelligence", *Mind* 59, no. 236 (1950): 433–460.

10   I explore this research in Chapter II.

There are two ways to explain this discovery. One explanation is that the computer needs a representation of the person to be simulated precisely because, being unlike a person, it needs guidance from a representation of what to simulate. This explanation presupposes that a real person doesn't need a representation of the person he is, because he already *is* that person. According to the alternative explanation, the reason why the computer needs guidance from a representation of the person to be simulated is that the person himself is guided by a representation of the person who he is. In other words, a computer simulates a person by coming to resemble him precisely in virtue of acting on a representation of him, as he does.

The latter explanation suggests that a person and a computer will pass the Turing Test in the very same way. Turing himself pointed out that his "imitation game" was often used as a test for humans rather than machines — for example, in a *viva voce* examination "to discover whether some one really understands something or has 'learnt it parrot fashion'."[11] Turing probably meant that a parrot cannot answer follow-up questions; yet a parrot that could answer follow-up questions would still answer "in parrot fashion" unless it had an objective self-conception. Let the examiner say, "Speak up, please", and the parrot would be stumped. In order to speak up when asked, the parrot would have to conceive of itself as a speaker in whom this request was intended to evoke a recognition (like this one) of the need to speak louder.[12]

Indeed, an objective self-conception is prerequisite to the simple speech act of telling someone something. Telling someone that *p* requires the intention that he believe *p* as a result of recognizing this very intention — an intention that contains a conception of oneself as the speaker and of itself as an intention that can be recognized.[13] Without that objective self-conception, we would be parrot-like communicators, squawking *at* one another rather than conversing *with* one another.

---

11   Turing, "Computing Machinery and Intelligence", 446.

12   Of course, an un-psittacine parrot would also need a second-person conception of his examiners. In addition to conceiving of *me* as "this creature", he would have to conceive of *those creatures* as "you". Whether the latter conception is possible without the former is another vexed question that, fortunately, need not be answered here.

13   This is Grice's analysis of assertion, in *Studies in the Ways of Words* (Cambridge, MA: Harvard University Press, 1989). Grice's analysis doesn't work as an analysis of assertion, since assertion doesn't necessarily involve the intention to be believed. Telling does involve that intention, however, and so it fits Grice's analysis.

Awareness vs. attention

My insistence on the role of an objective self-conception in personhood may seem to suggest that persons are continually thinking about themselves. No such thing is intended. The verb-phrase 'to think about' connotes not just awareness but attention, and self-directed attention is no part of the functions that I am describing.

Consider that you sometimes "forget yourself" in an activity, a phenomenon that Daoists call "non-action" and some psychologists call "flow".[14] When you forget yourself in an activity, you don't lose your first-personal awareness of performing it; what you lose is your objective awareness of yourself as the agent, an inhabitant of the world who is doing something and is hereby aware of doing it. In short, you lose your objective self-awareness. Since forgetting yourself in this sense is the exception, the rule must be remembering yourself — that is, maintaining your objective self-awareness.

Yet when you "remember yourself" in an activity, you aren't "thinking about" yourself, either; your objective self-awareness is merely implicit. On those very rare occasions when I wear a suit, I don't watch myself wearing the suit; I don't think, "Now I'll wear my suit across the street." But when I cross the street, I put the idea of crossing the street into action, and it isn't the idea of street-crossing in the abstract, or of someone or other's crossing the street; it's the idea of myself crossing the street, and the self in that idea is wearing a suit. So I tend to square my shoulders a bit, walk a bit slower, pull in my gut.

I sometimes forget about wearing a suit and plop down on the damp grass. What I have forgotten in that case is not anything that I was "thinking about" in most senses of the phrase; it's something of which I was merely, only implicitly aware. So until I forgot myself, my behavior was being guided by a whole lot more than I was thinking about in the sense that requires attention or explicit thought. One of the implicit thoughts by which it was guided is a conception of myself as a person presenting a well-dressed appearance that doesn't go well with a slouch.

---

14   I discuss this phenomenon, and its significance for the philosophy of action, in "The Way of the Wanton", in *Practical Identity and Narrative Agency*, ed. Kim Atkins and Catriona Mackenzie (New York: Routledge, 2008), 169–192.

Mutuality

An objective-self conception is essential to many forms of mutuality that are distinctive of persons. Consider joint intentions. When one intends to do something jointly with others, one must conceive of them as likewise intending to do it with oneself. Thinking of the other as so intending requires one to conceive of oneself as an agent with whom the other can intend to act, and to conceive of one's own intention as an intention that the other can thereby reciprocate. Joint intentions therefore require an objective self-conception.

Joint intentions are far more common than is generally noted by philosophers. They are essential even to the collective activity that consists in avoiding other collective activities. Subway riders intend to defuse bodily proximity by averting their eyes, but only if others intend likewise, since they intend to return unwanted stares, and they feel free to stare at others who aren't going to look anyway. Mutual neglect is also in force on a busy street, insofar as everyone intends to leave everyone else alone, provided that they intend likewise. Thus, joint intentions are operative even when people are doing nothing together besides doing nothing else together, and all of these joint intentions require objective self-awareness.

Like all objectively reflexive thought, joint intentions are self-referring. When I intend to do something on the condition of your intending likewise, "intending likewise" means having an intention with the same content as mine *mutatis mutandis*. The content of this intention depends on the content of its stipulation that you intend likewise, which depends in turn on the content of the whole intention. The content of my intention therefore yields a regress of contents depending on contents depending on contents, and so on *ad infinitum*.

The content of such an attitude is not finitely completable. Some regard this incompleteness as a problem, but I don't see why we cannot have attitudes with incompletable contents, so long as they have some content that is finitely complete. A British publisher used to place this notice on its copyright pages: "This book is sold subject to the condition that it shall not be lent, re-sold, hired out, or otherwise circulated without the publisher's prior consent and without a similar condition being imposed on the subsequent purchaser." No one was alarmed by the incompleteness of this condition.[15]

---

15   For discussion of this problem, including references, see the Appendix to my "How to Share an Intention", *Philosophy and Phenomenological Research* 57, no. 1 (1997): 29–50; reprinted in *The Possibility of Practical Reason*, 200–220.

Those alarmed by such cases are philosophers with a theory of attitudes and propositions — a theory almost universally accepted by philosophers but, I would say, in need of revision precisely because of its alarming implications.

An objective self-conception is required for joint *attention* as well as joint *intention*. When two people watch the sunset together, rather than merely side by side, each sees the sunset as being likewise seen by the other. You see the sunset as being seen also by the other, and as being seen by the other as being hereby seen by you. Your visual experience therefore represents you as seen by the other as having that very experience — an objectively reflexive representation.

Joint attention and joint intention are often combined. Imagine that you are viewing a painting in a museum while standing next to a stranger who is viewing the same painting. In your peripheral vision, you see him in front of the painting; you presume that he sees you in his peripheral vision as well. But you don't quite see whether he is looking at the painting. (For all you can see, he might be reading the legend next to it.) Or maybe you don't quite see whether he is seeing you look at the painting. (For all you can see, it might be the case for all he can see that you are reading the legend.) In short, you and he may have common knowledge of standing side by side in front of the painting, but you have not entered a state of joint attention to it.

Now imagine that you enter a state of joint attention. Each of you not only sees the painting but sees it as being likewise seen by the other, which entails its being seen by the other as being likewise seen by yourself. The representational contents of your visual experiences are now causally dependent on the direction of one another's gaze: those contents will change if the other looks away, since you will no longer see the painting as being jointly seen. Each party's visual experience is thus under the control of both gazes: what each sees is dependent on where both look.[16]

If you are visiting the museum with a companion, you probably have a joint intention to pay joint attention to the various paintings in turn. That is, each of you intends to join the other in viewing the next painting, but only while the other is like-minded; both intentions allow for breaking the

---

16 This change need not involve the sensory content of your visual experience — the arrangement of colors and shapes in your visual field. What changes is the representational content of the experience. This change in representational content may be experienced as a Gestalt switch, as the relations between the represented items are perceived to change.

joint view of the painting if either shows signs of intending to do so; and each intends to move on in that case, so long as the other intends likewise. So the direction of both gazes is determined by both intentions and, in turn, determines both visual experiences. Where each of you looks depends on where both of you intend to look, and where both of you look determines what each of you sees.

An objective self-conception may be essential to the distinctively human form of sexual arousal. Writing in a different context, Nagel says, "Sexual desire involves [...] not only perceptions of the sexual object, but perceptions of oneself."[17] He continues:

> [Romeo] notices, and moreover senses, Juliet sensing him [. . .] Juliet [. . .] senses that he senses her. This puts Romeo in a position to notice, and be aroused by, her arousal at being sensed by him. He senses that she senses that he senses her. This is still another level of arousal, for he becomes conscious of his sexuality through his awareness of its effect on her and of her awareness that this effect is due to him.

Obviously, Romeo can enter this erotic hall-of-mirrors only if he thinks of Juliet as aroused by his own arousal — a thought that requires an objective self-conception, of himself and his sexuality as sexual objects for her.

Of course, animals feel sexual arousal, and our sexual response has evolved from theirs. The point is that objectively reflexive thought is crucial to what has evolved. The reason why dogs aren't ashamed when seen mating is not that they are shameless, like exhibitionists; it's that they are utterly incapable of shame, because they cannot imagine being seen as failing to conceal themselves.[18] The kind of sexual arousal that Nagel describes — the kind that's distinctive of persons — involves the conception of oneself as exposed to the gaze of another in a state that would ordinarily be concealed.

Solitude

Finally, an objective self-conception is necessary for the distinctively human way of being alone, which Hannah Arendt characterized as solitude. "Solitude", she wrote, "means that though alone, I am together with somebody (myself, that is)."[19] In other words, solitude entails keeping oneself company.

---

17   "Sexual Perversion", *The Journal of Philosophy* 66 (1969): 10.
18   I discuss the emotion of shame in "The Genesis of Shame", *Philosophy & Public Affairs* 30, no. 1 (2001): 27–52; reprinted in *Self to Self: Selected Essays* (New York: Cambridge University Press, 2005), 45–69.
19   "Some Questions of Moral Philosophy", in *Responsibility and Judgment*, ed. Jerome Kohn (New York: Schocken Books, 2003), 49–146.

The capacity for solitude is what Donald Winnicott had in mind when he wrote that a child learns to be alone by being alone in the presence of another.[20] A child is alone in the presence of another when, instead of jointly attending to a toy or book, the child and the other attend to separate activities while remaining jointly aware of one another's presence. The child then acquires the ability to lie snugly in bed aware of his parents talking softly downstairs aware of him lying upstairs snugly in bed. From there he can make the transition to solitude, because his awareness of his parents' awareness of him has led him to notice that he is someone there in bed, someone who can keep him company in bed, hence that he can keep himself company.

None of these instances of objective self-awareness involves self-directed attention or explicit thought. One can watch the sunset in solitude without focusing on oneself, but if one weren't aware of being by oneself, and of being hereby aware of that fact, one wouldn't be watching in solitude; if one is to watch in company with another, being one of the company must enter one's awareness, even though the sunset has one's undivided attention; when working with another on a joint project, one attends to the project, but if it is truly to be a joint project, then one must conceive of oneself as a member of the reciprocally intending pair; and that goes as well for the pair whose joint project unfolds in bed. Thus, objective self-awareness is central to many settings, both solitary and social, where explicitly thinking about oneself would be out of place.

Valuing Objective Self-Awareness

I have tried to show that an objective self-conception is crucial to a wide variety of functions that are characteristic of persons. The list now includes central elements of rational agency, such as perceiving an open future and planning for it. It also includes distinctively personal forms of apartness (solitude), togetherness (companionship), and interaction (conversation, sex). I now turn to various ways in which we value personhood conceived as the capacity for these distinctive functions. My first example of valuing personhood was Thomas Nagel's amazement at being a particular person. It is now time to face the question: What is so amazing?

What amazes Nagel about being a particular person, recall, is that he is "anything so [. . .] concrete and specific". This amazement at his own

---

20 "The Capacity to Be Alone", in *The Maturational Processes and the Facilitating Environment: Studies in the Theory of Emotional Development* (London: Karnac Books, 1990), 29–36.

concrete specificity must have a foil in something else about himself with which it contrasts. What is it about himself that makes Nagel's concrete specificity so amazing to him?

Nagel himself contrasts his concrete specificity with the size and grandeur of the universe. He says:[21]

> I begin by considering the world as a whole, as if from nowhere, and in those vast spaces TN is just one person among countless others, all equally insignificant. Taking up that impersonal standpoint produces in me a sense of complete detachment from TN. How can I, who am thinking about the entire, centerless universe, be anything so specific as this: this measly creature existing in a tiny morsel of space and time, with a definite and by no means universal mental and physical organization? How can I be anything so small and concrete and specific?

There are two contrasts at work in this passage. The first is a contrast in size, between the vastness of the universe and the "tiny morsel of space and time" that Nagel occupies. To my mind, however, the crucial contrast is the second, which is between the centerlessness of the universe and Nagel's "definite and by no means universal [. . .] organization". Centerlessness is a feature of the infinite — there is no median integer — whereas Nagel is finite, or as he puts it, "definite and by no means universal". What amazes Nagel is that this by-no-means-universal creature can be thinking about the centerlessly infinite universe, can encompass the universe *in thought*. The wonder, in other words, is that a concrete and specific individual can think abstractly about everything there is. And the shameless megalomania to which Nagel nearly confesses would be based on the assumption that only "the world soul" could contain such an idea.

There is indeed something remarkable about the capacity of a concrete individual to quantify abstractly over everything — something remarkable, that is, about the disproportion between the universality of the quantifier and the particularity of the creature who thinks it. That disproportion is what amazes Nagel, I believe, as he shifts attention from the universe to his measly self.

Nagel could have felt magnified rather than diminished by the disproportion. And he could have been impressed by the even more remarkable disproportion between his own finitude and his infinitely regressive thoughts, which themselves partake of infinitude, albeit abstractly, in the determination of their content. That is, he could have

---

21   Nagel, "The Objective Self", *op. cit.*, 225.

been impressed by his capacity to have thoughts whose content implicitly involves the incompletably many iterations of self-reference.

A person has what you might call psychic depth.[22] The description of someone's eyes as deep pools is trite but not, for all that, untrue. What we see when we look into someone's eyes is his self-awareness, because we see him seeing us likewise, hence seeing us seeing him, *ad infinitum* — a regress in which he goes on endlessly seeing himself being seen. If we are paying proper attention, we marvel at the bottomless depth of the self-awareness that is embodied in this particular, concrete human being. If only Nagel had concentrated on his capacity for such self-awareness rather than the measly creature who has it, he would have been impressed by himself for being a person.

Love

We don't have a word for this sense of wonder at personhood, but we do have a word for an emotion of which it is often a part. It is often a part of love.[23]

When we philosophers talk about love, we are almost always talking about a twine of attitudes and dispositions, strands of which may include attraction, affection, attachment — plus identification, sympathy, benevolence — also loyalty, gratitude, pity — not to mention nostalgia and pride. The reason why we are talking about many of these things at once is that we are usually talking about our feelings for people whom we would describe as loved ones: friends, family, lovers. In the context of these relationships, I would say, love is more of a syndrome than a single emotion.

So I don't see much point in talking about what love *is*. Still, I think that there is one strand of emotion that almost always runs through love and

---

22 Personhood involves many dimensions of psychic depth, of course. Charles Taylor explains "our ordinary use of the metaphor of depth applied to people" in terms of how a person evaluates his own motives. See "What Is Human Agency?", in *The Self: Psychological and Philosophical Issues*, ed. Theodore Mischel (Oxford: Blackwell, 1977), 114 ff. In this sense, only some people are deep. But being either deep or shallow in this sense requires objective self-awareness, which makes all persons deep in my sense.

23 This section expands upon my previous writings about love: "Love as a Moral Emotion", *Ethics* 109, no. 2 (1999): 338–374, and "Beyond Price", *Ethics* 118, no. 2 (2008): 191–212. The first is reprinted in *Self to Self: Selected Essays* (New York: Cambridge University Press, 2005), 70–109.

for which we have no other term: it's the emotion that I have described as amazement at the personhood of another.

Asya Passinsky has independently arrived at a similar view, based on Kant's theory of the sublime. She believes that love is an experience of the beloved as sublime — specifically, as mathematically sublime, in the sense defined by Kant.

Kant says that our sense of the sublime involves "a representation of *limitlessness*, yet with the super-added thought of its totality".[24] We experience the sublime when a magnitude outruns the capacity of our imagination but can be encompassed by our reason, as when we find that we cannot count to infinity but can grasp it intellectually. We feel displeasure when the imagination despairs of reaching the infinite and pleasure when reason triumphs in grasping it. The tension between pleasure and displeasure generates our sense of the sublime, according to Kant.

In my view, the limitlessness of the beloved is to be found in his capacity for objectively reflexive thoughts, with their implicit regress of self-reference. The totality of this unimaginable regress is represented not just in our intellectual grasp of the regress itself but in our grasp of its being implicit in thoughts entertained by a concrete, specific individual. When we register the tension between this limitlessness and its totality, we have an experience of the sublime, and that experience amounts to a component of love.

(It stands to reason that the experience I am describing should be the experience of the sublime, given that it is the inverse of Nagel's sense of being a measly little creature, which might be described as the experience of the ridiculous.)[25]

The mere knowledge of someone's personhood is not an emotional matter: before one can get emotional about someone's personhood, one has to notice and pay attention to it. Even when Nagel is not attending to the fact that he is TN, he is certainly aware of it. He isn't amazed, however, until

---

24   *The Critique of Judgment*, trans. James Creed Meredith (Oxford: Clarendon Press, 1952), Book II, §23, Acad. 244, 90.

25   In his essay on the absurd, Nagel writes: "[H]umans have the special capacity to step back and survey themselves, and the lives to which they are committed, with that detached amazement which comes from watching an ant struggle up a heap of sand. Without developing the illusion that they are able to escape from their highly specific and idiosyncratic position, they can view it *sub specie aeternitatis* — and the view is at once sobering and comical." "The Absurd", *The Journal of Philosophy* 68 (1971): 720.

he confronts his personhood face-to-face. He marvels at being a particular person only when he attends to the contrast between his finite particularity and his infinitely recursive thoughts.

Similarly with our appreciation of one another's personhood. We can look one another in the eye without consciously registering that we are seeing and being seen *like this* and that our visual experience is therefore incompletably recursive in content — more colloquially, that both of us are looking into bottomless pools.

Sometimes, though, mutual awareness is not necessary to seeing someone as self-aware. Some people just strike us as *there* in their faces, as if the lights are on and there's somebody home. We almost never speak to them, much less become acquaintances, even less friends. If, against all odds, we become lovers, however, we will say that it was love at first sight, and we won't be guilty of retrospective projection. At first sight we really did feel an important part of what we will feel then.

People scoff at the idea of love at first sight. They are right to scoff if the idea is that a single look can provoke the entire syndrome; they are wrong if they think that it cannot provoke an important component of the syndrome — an important strand even if not the whole ball of twine.

Friendship

The amazement of love is not our only evaluative response to the personhood of others. We also value personhood in appreciating the personhood of our friends.

Aristotle's theory of friendship includes a role for companionship and joint intention. He starts out by describing friendship as "two going together",[26] and he later contrasts the case of people living together with "the case of cattle, grazing in the same place".[27] When cattle merely graze in the same place, they are not grazing together, because they are not jointly aware of doing so. They are like children engaged in what we call parallel play.

Visiting a museum is a human sort of grazing, but visiting with a companion is not just a case of grazing in the same place, or parallel play; it's a case of two going together. The point of visiting the museum with a companion is to join in viewing the paintings out of a joint intention so

---

26 *Nicomachean Ethics*, ed. and trans. Roger Crisp (Cambridge: Cambridge University Press, 2000), VIII.i, 143.

27 *Ibid.*, IX.ix, 179.

to view them, thereby having a shared activity and a shared experience. Although you naturally prefer some friends over others as partners in museum-going, and you prefer friends over strangers, grazing the galleries with a companionable stranger may be preferable to going alone. The mere personhood of another person, which makes him eligible for going together, is of value even in the absence of any personal relationship. And conversely, one of the many values in personal relationships is that they provide ready access to companionship of the kind that you would value even in a companionable stranger.

Solitude

Another way of valuing personhood is to take pleasure in solitude. Pleasure taken in one's own company does not come from finding oneself entertaining. Entertaining oneself, keeping oneself occupied, are distractions from solitude. The pleasure of solitude comes from simply contemplating one's capacity for being company to someone — in this case, oneself. It thus comes from appreciating one's own personhood.

Sometimes one's own company is not enough, and then the awareness of having only oneself for company turns from solitude into loneliness. One longs for more company, which would be an enlargement of one's own. What one longs for, in other words, is to enlarge one's solitary self-awareness to include the shared self-awareness involved in joint attention, joint intention, and other forms of mutuality. One thereby appreciates the value of what one is missing, the personhood of others, and also the unrealized potential in oneself, which consists in one's own personhood.

So there are many ways in which humans value personhood: love and sexual arousal; pleasure in solitude, in companionship, and in friendship; loneliness. These ways of valuing personhood are mutually reinforcing, both dispositionally and occurrently. The capacity to savor solitude enhances one's capacities for companionship, friendship, and love; loving someone in particular enhances friendship and companionship with him, and of course sex as well.

I think that a similar function is served by the much-derided phenomenon of love at first sight. The amazement that can turn out to have been the beginning of love usually leads nowhere but still alerts one to the value at which full-blown love would stand in wonder. Feeling incipient love for a perfect stranger thus enlivens one's capacity for appreciating personhood in other ways. It may be followed by reflective solitude or depressing loneliness or the thought of a real-life lover, all of which are further ways of valuing personhood.

Valuing Personhood

I have tried to show that these evaluative responses have as their objects manifestations of the same phenomenon, namely, the objective self-conception that makes persons the amazing creatures we are. I hope you will agree that the responses I have catalogued are not culture-bound. Enjoying both solitude and companionship, suffering from loneliness, being wowed by a beloved, feeling the buzz of mutual arousal — these responses aren't peculiar to any place or time. They are rooted in human nature.

In calling these responses natural, I do not mean to imply that they are naturally selected. I don't think that valuing manifestations of objectively reflexive thought is necessarily adaptive, but then, I don't think that evolutionary theory is the place to look for what is moral in human nature. All I claim is that valuing personhood is a part of human nature — witness the way it figures in the universally human ways of being together and being alone. It appears to come along with the cognitive capacity for objectively reflexive thought, which may itself have been adaptive for other reasons.[28]

Because these evaluative responses are rooted in human nature, they constrain the ways of life on which human beings are likely to converge — provided, of course, that they are free to converge spontaneously, rather than herded together by powerful individuals or interest groups. Left to coordinate on their own, members a human community will favor ways of life that are hospitable to valuing persons as humans naturally do — hospitable, that is, to the uninhibited enjoyment of solitude, companionship, friendship, love, and sex. Such ways of life are unlikely to be moral black holes.

---

28 In "What Good is a Will?" (*Action in Context*, ed. Anton Leist [Berlin/New York: Walter de Gruyter/Mouton, 2007], 193–215), I discuss the possibility that rational agency is an evolutionary spandrel — that is, a product of adaptations but not itself an adaptation.

VI. Life Absurd? Don't Be Ridiculous

Macbeth says that life is a tale told by an idiot, signifying nothing. This description fits Thomas Nagel's definition of absurdity: "a conspicuous discrepancy between pretension or aspiration and reality".[1] Nagel offers his own examples: "[S]omeone gives a complicated speech in support of a motion that has already been passed; a notorious criminal is made president of a major philanthropic foundation; you declare your love over the telephone to a recorded announcement; as you are being knighted, your pants fall down." We might add: "An idiot tells a tale that signifies nothing." The idiot aspires or pretends to tell a tale, and he talks nonsense instead.

Yet Macbeth's metaphor suggests that Nagel's definition of absurdity is off the mark. In Macbeth's metaphor, what is absurd is not the idiot's pretense of telling a tale; what's absurd is the tale itself: it signifies nothing. An idiot's attempt to tell a tale is not absurd; it's ridiculous — worthy of ridicule, derision, mockery. Similarly with Nagel's examples. If your pants fall down in front of the Queen, it's ridiculous, not absurd.

Nagel dismisses the traditional tropes of life's absurdity:

> It is often remarked that nothing we do now will matter in a million years. But if that is true, then by the same token, nothing that will be the case in a million years matters now. In particular, it does not matter now that in a million years nothing we do now will matter. (11)

As much as I enjoy seeing Nagel turn the tables on this cliché, I think that his reasoning is flawed. True enough, facts about the remote future are of no importance in the present, but Nagel is talking about facts that aren't strictly about the future; they're about the relation between the future and the present. The latter facts are about the present, too, and so they matter already. I would be thrilled to learn that this essay would still be

---

1 "The Absurd", *The Journal of Philosophy* 68 (1971): 718; also *Mortal Questions* (Cambridge: Cambridge University Press, 1979), 13.

DOI: 10.11647/OBP.0029.06

read a million years hence, but not because I would be thrilled about that future state of affairs in itself; the thrill would be the long-lastingness of my words, which would be a million-year-long fact, beginning now. I would of course be foolish to feel disappointed about not being read in a million years, but only because any such hope would be ridiculous. Again, a discrepancy between aspiration and reality yields ridiculousness, not absurdity.

Ultimately, Nagel improves on his initial definition of the absurd, by shifting his attention to a more pertinent discrepancy than that between pretension and reality. I will offer an interpretation of his ultimate conception of absurdity. Then I will consider how it gets played out in the metaethical debate over moral relativism, belief in which is sometimes thought to make life seem absurd.

The contradiction

Nagel appears to contradict himself at various points. On the one hand, he denies that the source of absurdity is our lack of a justification for taking things seriously. Such justifications are easy enough to find:

> No further justification is needed to make it reasonable to take aspirin for a headache, attend an exhibition of the work of a painter one admires, or stop a child from putting his hand on a hot stove. No larger context or further purpose is needed to prevent these acts from being pointless. (12)

On the other hand, Nagel says that the purpose of these actions is open to question — a kind of question that he compares to skeptical doubt:

> We can ask not only why we should believe there is a floor under us, but also why we should believe the evidence of our senses at all — and at some point, the frameable questions will have outlasted the answers. Similarly, we can ask not only why we should take aspirin, but why we should take trouble over our own comfort at all. (19)

These passages seem incompatible. How can we doubt whether to bother with our own comfort if, as the first passage assures us, no further purpose is needed?

The contradiction is not Nagel's, however; the contradiction is ours — and that is Nagel's point. His point is that "the absurdity of our situation derives not from a collision between our expectations and the world, but from a collision within ourselves" (17). Specifically, it derives from "the collision between the seriousness with which we take our lives and the perpetual possibility of regarding everything about which we are serious as arbitrary, or open to doubt" (13):

> These two inescapable viewpoints collide in us, and that is what makes life absurd. It is absurd because we ignore the doubts that we know cannot be settled, continuing to live with nearly undiminished seriousness in spite of them. (14)

We wonder why we should bother about our comfort, but then we go ahead and take an aspirin anyway.

These views come into collision because they do not just alternate; they coexist. We see the arbitrariness of our pursuits while still seriously engaged in them. "[W]hen we take this view and recognize what we do as arbitrary, it does not disengage us from life, and there lies our absurdity: not in the fact that such an external view can be taken of us, but in the fact that we ourselves can take it, without ceasing to be the persons whose ultimate concerns are so coolly regarded" (15).[2]

Nagel illustrates the point by imagining what would happen if a mouse became self-aware:

> If that did happen, his life would become absurd, since self-awareness would not make him cease to be a mouse and would not enable him to rise above his mousely strivings. Bringing his new-found self-consciousness with him, he would have to return to his meagre yet frantic life, full of doubts that he was unable to answer, but also full of purposes that he was unable to abandon. (21)

Thus, absurdity lies not where the pretension involved in taking things seriously collides with the reality of their arbitrariness; it lies rather in our seeing the collision and continuing to take things seriously all the same. To revise Nagel's initial examples, we are like a person who continues to speak in favor of a motion not just after it has been passed but after having realized that it has been passed; we are like a person who continues a marriage proposal after having recognized the voice on the other end of the line as a recording.

Thus revised, these examples succeed in illustrating absurdity after all. Indeed, they illustrate absurdity snatched from the jaws of ridiculousness. If a speaker perseveres after having realized that his speech is ridiculous, he can turn his audience's laughter into puzzlement at the absurdity of his

---

2 "And that is the main condition of absurdity — the dragooning of an unconvinced transcendent consciousness into the service of an immanent, limited enterprise like a human life" (726).

performance. Nagel's corresponding vision of human life can be restated as follows: Taking our arbitrary pursuits so seriously would be ridiculous if not for the fact that we know they are arbitrary, so that our seriousness is absurd instead.

Arbitrariness

Notice that Nagel describes our ordinary pursuits as both arbitrary and open to doubt. He doesn't distinguish between these conditions, but they are not the same. We need to consider how arbitrariness and doubt are related to one another and how both are related to absurdity.

Arbitrariness and doubt

The concept of arbitrariness properly applies to a decision taken on no basis whatsoever, without justification. But there are two ways for a decision to be baseless, and only one of them leads to doubt. On the one hand, we may be unable to provide a justification where one is called for, and so our decision may be subject to a standard of success or correctness that we cannot show it to meet. Then our decision is open to doubt. On the other hand, there may be no applicable standard, hence no call for justification. The invitation to pick a number from one to ten presupposes that there is no correct answer, and so our choice, though arbitrary, will not be open to doubt.

Nagel is speaking of choices that seem to need justification, hence to be threatened by arbitrariness of the first kind. Yet that threat does not appear to be realized in these cases, because our choices are not baseless after all:

> [H]uman beings do not act solely on impulse. They are prudent, they reflect, they weigh consequences, they ask whether what they are doing is worth while. Not only are their lives full of particular choices that hang together in larger activities with temporal structure: they also decide in the broadest terms what to pursue and what to avoid, what the priorities among their various aims should be, and what kind of people they want to be or become. [. . .] They spend enormous quantities of energy, risk, and calculation on the details. (14–15)

Because these choices are made on the basis of reasons, they are not arbitrary. So where does arbitrariness come in? How can Nagel say that our pursuits are arbitrary while also saying that they are guided by such painstaking deliberation?

Maybe arbitrariness enters because deliberation and justification must come to a stop at some point, and the stopping point is necessarily arbitrary: it cannot itself be a matter of deliberation or justification, lest they go on forever. Maybe, then, the arbitrariness lies in our choice of when to stop looking for reasons.

Yet Nagel says that there is a point, a non-arbitrary point, at which we feel no need for further reasons. "[J]ustifications come to an end," Nagel says, "when we are content to have them end — when we do not find it necessary to look any further" (16). Here we have reached "[t]he things we do or want without reasons, and without requiring reasons — the things that define what is a reason for us and what is not" (19). We are content to have justification end at this point "because of the way we are put together; what seems to us important or serious or valuable would not seem so if we were differently constituted" (17–18).

So we do not arbitrarily decide to stop demanding justifications; we simply hit the bedrock of our own constitution. We stop because we see that justifications cannot go on forever and it is in our constitution to be content with the justifications already in hand.

The question therefore returns: Where is the arbitrariness? Here is another possibility: Maybe what's arbitrary is our constitution, the bedrock that brings justifications to an end:[3]

> This explains why the sense of absurdity finds its natural expression in those bad arguments with which the discussion began. Reference to our small size and short lifespan and to the fact that all of mankind will eventually vanish without a trace are metaphors for the backward step which permits us to regard ourselves from without and to find the particular form of our lives curious and slightly surprising. By feigning a nebula's-eye view, we illustrate the capacity to see ourselves without presuppositions, as arbitrary, idiosyncratic, highly specific occupants of the world, one of countless possible forms of life. (21)

But how can the human form of life be arbitrary? If we know that justifications must come to an end somewhere, and if we are satisfied with

---

3 Nagel makes clear that he is concerned with human life in general rather than particular lives: "Many people's lives are absurd, temporarily or permanently, for conventional reasons having to do with their particular ambitions, circumstances, and personal relations. If there is a philosophical sense of absurdity, however, it must arise from the perception of something universal — some respect in which pretension and reality inevitably clash for us all" (718).

justifications that end with our constitution as humans, then where is the unsatisfied demand that makes for arbitrariness?

Arbitrariness and specificity

In the end, I think, Nagel doesn't mean that human life is arbitrary, strictly speaking. He is using the term, I suspect, as if it were equivalent to the other terms on his list, such as "idiosyncratic" and "highly specific". That these other terms are his real concern is suggested in another passage:

> [H]umans have the special capacity to step back and survey themselves, and the lives to which they are committed, with that detached amazement which comes from watching an ant struggle up a heap of sand. Without developing the illusion that they are able to escape from their highly specific and idiosyncratic position, they can view it *sub specie aeternitatis* — and the view is at once sobering and comical. (15)

Nagel returns to this topic in an essay published more than ten years after his essay on the absurd. There he expresses a sense of wonderment at his own personal specificity:[4]

> [H]ow can I be merely a particular person? The problem here is not how it can be the case that I am this one rather than that one, but how I can be anything as specific as a particular person in the world — any person.

In these passages, Nagel seems to conflate particularity with specificity, and specificity in turn with peculiarity. That is, he seems to presuppose that a particular thing, numerically distinct from other particulars, must have some combination of qualities by which it can specified — qualities specific or peculiar to it, idiosyncrasies. And then he seems to equate having such peculiarities with being odd, strange, alien. Thus, he says that despite taking an external perspective from which we become spectators of our lives, "we continue to lead them, and devote ourselves to what we are able at the same time to view as no more than a curiosity, like the ritual of an alien religion" (20–21). The rituals of an alien religion are peculiar in the sense that they are encrusted with details that are specific to them and therefore odd to outsiders. What Nagel finds absurd, then, is the collision between the seriousness with which we take our lives and the

---

4   "The Objective Self", in *Knowledge and Mind: Philosophical Essays*, ed. Carl Ginet and Sydney Shoemaker (New York: Oxford University Press, 1983), 212.

simultaneous awareness that human life is peculiar, strange, one among countless possible forms of life.

Yet if the seriousness with which we take our lives somehow clashes with an awareness of their peculiarity, then it must somehow incorporate a pretension or aspiration not to be peculiar, not strange, not specific in Nagel's sense. Taking things seriously must then entail aspiring to be creatures-in-general — beings without peculiar qualities, like God. That aspiration would be ridiculous, as Nagel himself sees:[5]

> I know this sounds like metaphysical megalomania of an unusually shameless kind. Merely being TN isn't good enough for me: I have to think of myself as the world soul in humble disguise.

So maybe human life is absurd only if we are being ridiculous.

Transcending Specificity

That's unfair. There is a familiar view that involves an aspiration to transcend specificity: it's called absolutism about value. The absolutist doesn't necessarily pretend to transcend specificity, but he does aspire to, for he aspires to value things that are simply to-be-valued, irrespective of contingent variations among valuers. Pursuing things of absolute value would be a form of life that isn't idiosyncratic or peculiar: it would be the one and only Way to Live.

It's as if there is one God whom all spiritual creatures are trying to worship and will end up worshipping alike at the ideal end of spiritual evolution. Different beings may perform different rituals, encrusted with their own peculiarities, but all are earnestly striving to shed those peculiarities, in the conviction that God demands to be worshipped in just one way. Similarly, according to the absolutist, things demand to be valued in just one way, and taking things seriously consists in striving to value them as they demand, thus striving not to be peculiar.

If there is such a thing as absolute value, then there is nothing ridiculous about this kind of seriousness, which aspires to transcend human idiosyncrasy in valuing. Nor is life absurd in the eyes of someone who believes in the possibility of such transcendence: he sees no collision between his pretensions and reality. Only someone who doubts that

---

5 *Ibid.*, 225.

possibility might find his life absurd — that is, if he cannot moderate his aspirations accordingly.

Those of us who are relativists about value must regard our lives, and human life in general, as inevitably specific and idiosyncratic. We don't believe in a universally valid Way to Live to which all creatures can aspire; we believe that every creature has to live its own peculiar life. We are like observant nonbelievers, knowing that there is no one true religion but still earnestly performing our rituals simply because they are ours. And isn't nonbelieving observance a bit absurd?

When it comes to the human form of life, which appears to be Nagel's concern, the answer is clear. Of course humans are a specific kind of creature, specifiably different from other kinds, hence idiosyncratic among all creatures. Of course, then, there are humanly valuable things that aren't valuable in some nonspecific way. But we are content to be human — what else could we be? — and so we can be human seriously. If absolutists aspire to trans-humanity, then they go above and beyond the call of seriousness.

The question becomes more pressing when applied, within the category of human life, to its more specific cultural and individual forms. I know that my upper-middle-class American way of life, and my own personal pursuits, are specific and idiosyncratic in relation to the countless possibilities. Does that knowledge clash with my taking them seriously? No. I don't aspire to be Everyman: being David Velleman is enough for me, no matter how peculiar I may look from another point of view. Like Nagel, I am gripped by the question "How could I be a particular person?", but whereas the question appears to fill Nagel with anxiety, it fills me with wonder.

Moral Seriousness

But what, at last, about moral seriousness? In the eyes of many philosophers, moral seriousness requires the conviction that what we call morality is not merely *our* morality, not just a set of *mores* peculiar to our culture or community. If these philosophers are right, then moral relativism implies that our lives are absurd, given our inability to abandon moral seriousness. This threatened absurdity is the *absurdum* in the widely accepted *reductio* of relativism.

I don't believe that moral relativism clashes with moral seriousness. Sufficient for moral seriousness is a belief in the possibility of progress in morality. In the context of moral relativism, of course, such progress cannot be progress toward a morality that better reflects transcendent moral truths. But there can still be progress toward a morality that better serves the function that moralities serve.

The view that there are different moralities specific to different communities suggests, may even entail, that all moralities share a common function; for on what other grounds would they share the title of moralities? And if specific moralities share a common function, then there is the possibility of their severally evolving in the direction of serving that function better. Each particular morality must evolve from what it already is, and there is no reason to assume that progress would bring particular moralities together in a moral consensus. They may always remain someone's morality, specific to a particular community, but they can still get better at doing what all moralities do. If we regard our own morality as embodying our progress to date, and we aspire to further progress, then we have all the moral seriousness we need, and it is compatible with recognizing that our morality is peculiar to us and potentially alien to others.

The idea is not that the function served by moralities is valuable: such a value would have to transcend the boundaries of any particular community. The idea is rather that having a morality belongs to the human form of life. It is in our constitution to form ourselves into communities with shared values and norms expressive of particular aspects of our humanity. So much is peculiar to human nature yet easy to take seriously simply because we are human. Given that peculiarity of human nature, progress in morality is possible, and so is moral seriousness in the form of aspiring to progress.

I conclude. The truth of moral relativism need not make life absurd. And because the pretensions of relativism are more modest than those of absolutism, believing relativism is less likely to be ridiculous.

Bibliography

Ardener, Edwin 1973. "'Behaviour': A Social Anthropological Criticism". *Journal of the Anthropological Society of Oxford* 4, no. 3: 152–154. Reprinted in *Journal for the Anthropological Study of Human Movement* 10 (1999): 139–141. Reprinted in Ardener, *The Voice of Prophecy and Other Essays*, ed. Malcolm Chapman Oxford: Blackwell, 1989.

— 1982. "Social Anthropology, Language and Reality". In *Semantic Anthropology*, ed. David Parkin, 1–14. New York: Academic Press.

Arendt, Hannah 2003. "Some Questions of Moral Philosophy". In *Responsibility and Judgment*, ed. Jerome Kohn, 49–146. New York: Schocken Books.

Aristotle 2000. *Nicomachean Ethics*, ed. and trans. Roger Crisp Cambridge: Cambridge University Press.

Basso, Keith H. 1970. "'To Give Up on Words': Silence in Western Apache Culture". *Southwestern Journal of Anthropology* 26, no. 5: 213–230.

Bicchieri, Cristina 2006. *The Grammar of Society: The Nature and Dynamics of Social Norms*. New York: Cambridge University Press.

Boghossian, Paul 2006. "What is Relativism?". In *Truth and Realism*, ed. Patrick Greenough and Michael P. Lynch, 13–37 Oxford: Oxford University Press.

— 2011. "Three Kinds of Relativism". In *A Companion to Relativism*, ed. Steven D. Hales, 53–69. Oxford: Wiley-Blackwell.

Bratman, Michael E. 1987. *Intention, Plans, and Practical Reason*. Cambridge, MA: Harvard University Press.

Broome, John 1991. *Weighing Goods*. Oxford: Blackwell.

— 1992. "Can a Humean Be Moderate?". In *Value, Welfare, and Morality*, ed. R.G. Frey and Christopher W. Morris, 51–73. Cambridge: Cambridge University Press.

Chung, Kyung-Sook 2006. "Korean Evidentials and Assertion". *Proceedings of the 25th West Coast Conference on Formal Linguistics*, ed. Donald Baumer, David Montero, and Michael Scanlon, 105–113. Somerville, MA: Cascadilla Proceedings Project. DOI: http://dx.doi.org/10.1016/j.lingua.2009.06.006.

Clark, Herbert H. 2006. "Social Actions, Social Commitments". In Enfield and Levinson (2006), 126–150.

Danziger, Eve 2006 "The Thought that Counts: Interactional Consequences of Variation in Cultural Theories of Meaning". In Enfield and Levinson (2006), 259–278.

Davidson, Donald 2001. *Inquiries into Truth and Interpretation*. Oxford: Clarendon Press.

— 1980. "Intending". In *Essays on Actions and Events*, 83–102. Oxford: Clarendon Press.

— 1973. "Radical Interpretation". *Dialectica* 27 (1973): 314–328. Reprinted in Davidson (2001).

Dennett, Daniel C. 1981. "Where Am I?". *Brainstorms: Philosophical Essays on Mind and Psychology*, 310–323. Cambridge, MA: The MIT Press.

Dostoyevsky, Fyodor 1954. "Something About Lying". In *The Diary of a Writer*, trans. Boris Brasol, 133–142. New York: George Braziller.

Dreier, James 1990. "Internalism and Speaker Relativism". *Ethics* 101, no. 1: 6–26.

du Boulay, Juliet 1976. "Lies, Mockery and Family Integrity". In *Mediterranean Family Structures*, ed. J.G. Peristiany, 389–406. Cambridge: Cambridge University Press.

Emerson, Ralph Waldo 1870. "Society and Solitude". In *Society and Solitude: Twelve Essays*. Cambridge, MA: The Riverside Press.

Enfield, N.J., and Stephen C. Levinson, eds., 2006. *Roots of Human Sociality: Culture, Cognition and Interaction*. New York: Berg.

Everett, Daniel L. 2008. *Don't Sleep, There Are Snakes: Life and Language in the Amazonian Jungle*. New York: Pantheon.

Faller, Martina T. 2002. *Semantics and Pragmatics of Evidentials in Cuzco Quechua*. Ph.D. dissertation submitted to the Department of Linguistics, Stanford University. http://personalpages.manchester.ac.uk/staff/martina.t.faller/documents/Thesis.pdf.

Fleck, David W. 2007. "Evidentiality and Double Tense in Matses". *Language* 83, no. 3: 589–614.

Foley, William A. 1997. *Anthropological Linguistics: An Introduction*. Malden, MA: Blackwell.

Franklin, S. 2003. "An Autonomous Software Agent for Navy Personnel Work: A Case Study in Human Interaction with Autonomous Systems in Complex Environments". In *Papers from 2003 AAAI Spring Symposium*, ed. D. Kortenkamp and M. Freed. Palo Alto: AAAI. Accessible at http://ccrg.cs.memphis.edu/papers.html.

Friedl, Ernestine 1962. *Vasilika: A Village in Modern Greece*. New York: Holt, Rinehart and Winston.

Geertz, Clifford 1960. *The Religion of Java*. Glencoe, IL: The Free Press.

— 1973. "Thick Description: Toward an Interpretive Theory of Culture". In *The Interpretation of Cultures*, 1–31. New York: Basic Books.

Gilbert, Margaret 1990. "Walking Together: A Paradigmatic Social Phenomenon". *Midwest Studies in Philosophy* 15: 1–14.

Gilsenan, Michael 1976. "Lying, Honor, and Contradiction". In *Transaction and Meaning: Directions in the Anthropology of Exchange and Symbolic Behavior*, ed. Bruce Kapferer. Philadelphia: Institute for the Study of Human Issues.

Goffman, Erving 1959. *The Presentation of Self in Everyday Life*. New York: Anchor Books.

Gombrich, Richard F. 1971. *Precept and Practice: Traditional Buddhism in the Rural Highlands of Ceylon*. Oxford: Clarendon Press.

Grice, H. Paul 1989. *Studies in the Ways of Words*. Cambridge, MA: Harvard University Press.

Harman, Gilbert 1976. "Practical Reasoning". *The Review of Metaphysics* 79, no. 3: 431–463.

— 1986. *Change in View: Principles of Reasoning*. Cambridge, MA: The MIT Press.

— 1986. "Willing and Intending". In *Philosophical Grounds of Rationality: Intentions, Categories, Ends*, ed. Richard E. Grandy and Richard Warner, 363–380. Oxford: Oxford University Press.

Harris, Rachael M. 1996. "Truthfulness, Conversational Maxims and Interaction in an Egyptian Village". *Transactions of the Philological Society* 94, no. 1: 31–55.

Hingley, Ronald 1977. *The Russian Mind*. New York: Charles Scribner's Sons.

Hume, David 1976. *A Treatise of Human Nature*, ed. L.A. Selby-Bigge, with text revised and notes by P.H. Nidditch. Oxford: Clarendon Press.

Kant, Immanuel 1952. *The Critique of Judgment*, trans James Creed Meredith. Oxford: Clarendon Press.

Keenan, Elinor Ochs 1976. "The Universality of Conversational Postulates". *Language in Society* 5, no. 1: 67–80.

Lewis, David 1969. *Convention: A Philosophical Study*. Cambridge, MA: Harvard University Press.

Loyall, A. Bryan 1997. *Believable Agents: Building Interactive Personalities*. Dissertation presented to the School of Computer Science, Carnegie Mellon University.

Mateas, Michael 1999. "An Oz-Centric View of Interactive Drama and Believable Agents". In *Artificial Intelligence Today: Recent Trends and Developments*, ed. Michael J. Wooldridge, 297–328. Berlin: Springer-Verlag.

Mill, John Stuart 1993. *Utilitarianism*. In *On Liberty and Utilitarianism*. New York: Bantam Books.

Nagel, Thomas 1969. "Sexual Perversion". *The Journal of Philosophy* 66: 5–17. Reprinted in Nagel (1979a), 39–52.

— 1971. "The Absurd". *The Journal of Philosophy* 68, no. 20: 716–727. Reprinted in Nagel (1979a), 11–23.

— 1979a. *Mortal Questions*. Cambridge: Cambridge University Press.

— 1979b. "Subjective and Objective". Nagel (1979a), 196–213.

— 1980. "The Limits of Objectivity". In *The Tanner Lectures on Human Values*, Vol. I, ed. Sterling M. McMurrin, 77–139. Salt Lake City: University of Utah Press.

— 1983. "The Objective Self". In *Knowledge and Mind: Philosophical Essays*, ed. Carl Ginet and Sydney Shoemaker, 211–232. New York: Oxford University Press.

— 1984. *The View From Nowhere*. New York: Oxford University Press.

— 1998. "Concealment and Exposure". *Philosophy & Public Affairs* 27, no. 1: 3–30.

Perry, John 1979. "The Problem of the Essential Indexical". *Noûs* 13, no. 1: 3–21. Reprinted in Perry (2000), 33–49.

— 1990. "Self-Notions". *Logos*: 17–31.

— 1998. "Myself and I". In *Philosophie in Synthetischer Absicht*, ed. Marcelo Stamm, 83–103. Stuttgart: Klett-Cotta.

— 2000. *The Problem of the Essential Indexical and Other Essays, Expanded Edition.* Stanford, CA: CSLI Publications.

Reisman, Karl 1989. "Contrapuntal Conversations in an Antiguan Village". In *Explorations in the Ethnography of Speaking*, ed. Richard Bauman and Joel Sherzer, 110–124. Cambridge: Cambridge University Press.

Rosaldo, Michelle 1982. "The Things We Do With Words: Ilongot Speech Acts and Speech Act Theory in Philosophy". *Language in Society* 11, no. 2: 203–237.

Ryle, Gilbert 1971. "The Thinking of Thoughts: What is 'Le Penseur' Doing?". *Collected Essays 1929–1968: Collected Papers Volume 2*, 480–496. London: Hutchinson.

Sacks, Harvey 1984. "On Doing 'Being Ordinary'". In *Structures of Social Action: Studies in Conversation Analysis*, ed. J. Maxwell Atkinson and John Heritage, 413–439. Cambridge: Cambridge University Press.

Sawyer, R. Keith 2001. *Creating Conversations: Improvisation in Everyday Discourse.* Cresskill, NJ: Hampton Press.

— 2003. *Improvised Dialogues: Emergence and Creativity in Conversation.* Westport, CT: Ablex Publishing.

Scanlon, T.M. 1999. *What We Owe to Each Other.* Cambridge, MA: Harvard University Press.

Schank, Roger C., and Robert P. Abelson 1977. *Scripts, Plans, Goals, and Understanding: An Inquiry Into Human Knowledge Structures.* Hillsdale, NJ: Lawrence Erlbaum Associates.

Schegloff, Emanuel A. 1996. "Confirming Allusions: Toward an Empirical Account of Action". *American Journal of Sociology* 102, no. 1: 161–216.

Schutz, Alfred 1953. "Common-Sense and Scientific Interpretation of Human Action". *Philosophy and Phenomenological Research* 14, no. 1: 1–38.

— 1954. "Concept and Theory Formation in the Social Sciences". *The Journal of Philosophy* 51, no. 9: 257–273.

— 1964. "Equality and the Meaning Structure of the Social World". *Collected Papers II*, ed. Arvid Brodersen, 226–273. The Hague: Martinus Nijhof.

Searle, John R., and Daniel Vanderveken 1985. *Foundations of Illocutionary Logic.* Cambridge: Cambridge University Press.

Searles, Ned 2000. "'Why Do You Ask So Many Questions?': Dialogical Anthropology and Learning How Not to Ask in Canadian Inuit Society". *Journal for the Anthropological Study of Human Movement* 11, no. 1: 47–64.

Senft, Gunter 2008. "The Case: The Trobriand Islanders vs H.P. Grice: Kilivila and the Gricean Maxims of Quality and Manner". *Anthropos* 103: 139–147.

Shoemaker, Sydney 1976. "Embodiment and Behavior". In *The Identities of Persons*, ed. Amélie Oksenberg Rorty, 109–137. Berkeley, CA: University of California Press.

Shweder, Richard A. 1990. "Ethical Relativism: Is There a Defensible Version?". *Ethos* 18, no. 2: 205–218.

Smith, Matthew Noah 2010. "Practical Imagination and Its Limits". *Philosophers' Imprint* 10, no. 3. http://hdl.handle.net/2027/spo.3521354.0010.003.

Street, Sharon (forthcoming). "Objectivity and Truth: You'd Better Rethink It".

— (in progress). "How to Be a Relativist About Normativity".

Sweetser, Eve E. 1987. "The Definition of *Lie*: An Examination of the Folk Models Underlying a Semantic Prototype". In *Cultural Models in Language and Thought*, ed. Dorothy Holland and Naomi Quinn, 43–66. Cambridge: Cambridge University Press.

Swidler, Ann 1986. "Culture in Action: Symbols and Strategies". *American Sociological Review* 51, no. 2: 273–286.

Taylor, Charles 1997. "What Is Human Agency?". In *The Self: Psychological and Philosophical Issues*, ed. Theodore Mischel, 103–135. Oxford: Blackwell.

Telban, Borut 2008. "The Poetics of the Crocodile: Changing Cultural Perspectives in Ambonwari". *Oceania* 78, no. 2: 217–235.

Thomas, Frank, and Ollie Johnston 1971. *Disney Animation: The Illusion of Life*. New York: Abbeville Press.

Turing, Alan 1950. "Computing Machinery and Intelligence". *Mind* 59, no. 236: 433–460.

Tversky, Amos, and Daniel Kahneman 1981. "The Framing of Decisions and the Psychology of Choice". *Science* 211, no. 4481: 453–458. DOI: 10.1126/science.7455683.

Velleman, J. David 1989a. "Epistemic Freedom". *Pacific Philosophical Quarterly* 70, no. 1: 73–97. Reprinted in Velleman (2009), 32–55.

— 1989b. *Practical Reflection*. Princeton, NJ: Princeton University Press.

— 1993. "The Story of Rational Action". *Philosophical Topics* 21, no. 1: 229–253. Reprinted in Velleman (2009), 144–169.

— 1997. "How to Share an Intention". *Philosophy and Phenomenological Research* 57, no. 1: 29–50. Reprinted in Velleman (2009), 200–220.

— 1999. "Love as a Moral Emotion". *Ethics* 109, no. 2: 338–274. Reprinted in Velleman (2006), 45–67.

— 2000. "From Self-Psychology to Moral Philosophy". *Philosophical Perspectives 14: Action and Freedom*: 349–377. Reprinted in Velleman (2005).

— 2001. "The Genesis of Shame". *Philosophy & Public Affairs* 30, no. 1: 27–52. Reprinted in Velleman (2006), 45–69.

— 2002. "Motivation by Ideal". *Philosophical Explorations* 5, no. 2: 89–103. Reprinted in Velleman (2005). DOI: 10.1080/10002002058538724.

— 2005. *Self to Self: Selected Essays*. New York: Cambridge University Press.

— 2007. "What Good is a Will?". In *Action in Context*, ed. Anton Leist, 193–215. Berlin/New York: Walter de Gruyter/Mouton.

— 2008a. "Beyond Price". *Ethics* 118, no. 2: 191–212.

— 2008b. "The Way of the Wanton". In *Practical Identity and Narrative Agency*, ed. Kim Atkins and Catriona Mackenzie, 169–192. New York: Routledge.

— 2009a. *How We Get Along*. New York: Cambridge University Press.

— 2009b. *The Possibility of Practical Reason*. Ann Arbor, MI: MPublishing.

von Fintel, Kai, and Lisa Matthewson 2008. "Universals in Semantics". *The Linguistic Review* 25, no. 1–2: 139–201. DOI: 10.1515/TLIR.2008.004.

Walton, Kendall L. 1990. *Mimesis as Make-Believe: On the Foundations of the Representational Arts*. Cambridge, MA: Harvard University Press.

Wierzbicka, Anna 1985. "A Semantic Metalanguage for a Crosscultural Comparison of Speech Acts and Speech Genres". *Language in Society* 14, no. 4: 491–514.

— 2009. "All People Eat and Drink. Does This Mean That 'Eat' and 'Drink' are Universal Human Concepts?". In *The Linguistics of Eating and Drinking*, ed. John Newman, 65–89. Amsterdam: John Benjamins.

Williams, Bernard 1982. "Internal and External Reasons". In *Moral Luck*, 101–113. Cambridge: Cambridge University Press.

Williams, Drid 1980. "Taxonomies of the Body". *Journal for the Anthropological Study of Human Movement* 1, no. 1: 1–11.

Winnicott, Donald 1990. "The Capacity to Be Alone". In *The Maturational Processes and the Facilitating Environment: Studies in the Theory of Emotional Development*, 29–36. London: Karnac Books.

Wong, David 2006. *Natural Moralities: A Defense of Pluralistic Relativism*. Oxford: Oxford University Press.

Wooldridge, Michael J. 2000. *Reasoning About Rational Agents*. Cambridge, MA: The MIT Press.

Index

This book does not end here...

At Open Book Publishers, we are changing the nature of the traditional academic book. The title you have just read will not be left on a library shelf, but will be accessed online by hundreds of readers each month across the globe. We make all our books free to read online so that students, researchers and members of the public who can't afford a printed edition can still have access to the same ideas as you.

Our digital publishing model also allows us to produce online supplementary material, including extra chapters, reviews, links and other digital resources. Find *Foundations for Moral Relativism* on our website to access its online extras. Please check this page regularly for ongoing updates, and join the conversation by leaving your own comments:

http://www.openbookpublishers.com/product/181

If you enjoyed this book, and feel that research like this should be available to all readers, regardless of their income, please think about donating to us. Our company is run entirely by academics, and our publishing decisions are based on intellectual merit and public value rather than on commercial viability. We do not operate for profit and all donations, as with all other revenue we generate, will be used to finance new Open Access publications.

For further information about what we do, how to donate to OBP, additional digital material related to our titles or to order our books, please visit our website.

OpenBook Publishers

Knowledge is for sharing

Lightning Source UK Ltd.
Milton Keynes UK
UKOW051928070413

208823UK00004B/7/P